MW00612431

simple
SMALL-BATCH
baking

simple
SMALL-BATCH
baking

60 Recipes for Perfectly Portioned
Cookies, Cakes, Bars, *and More*

MIKE JOHNSON

Author of *Even Better Brownies*

PAGE STREET
PUBLISHING CO.

PAGE STREET
PUBLISHING CO.

Copyright © 2022 Michael Johnson

First published in 2022 by
Page Street Publishing Co.
27 Congress Street, Suite 1511
Salem, MA 01970
www.pagestreetpublishing.com

All rights reserved. No part of this book may be reproduced or used, in any form or by any means, electronic or mechanical, without prior permission in writing from the publisher.

Distributed by Macmillan, sales in Canada by The Canadian Manda Group.

26 25 24 23 22   1 2 3 4 5

ISBN-13: 978-1-64567-644-7
ISBN-10: 1-64567-644-7

Library of Congress Control Number: 2022938804

Cover and book design by Rosie Stewart for Page Street Publishing Co.
Photography by Michael Johnson

Printed and bound in the United States

Page Street Publishing protects our planet by donating to nonprofits like The Trustees, which focuses on local land conservation.

DEDICATION

To my family and friends, for being my biggest
supporters and the best taste testers.

CONTENTS

INTRODUCTION

We've all been there . . . when that sweet-tooth craving hits, but you don't want to commit to making three dozen cookies or a tray of brownies large enough to feed the neighborhood. Sometimes you just want a teeny Funfetti® cake, a bit of chocolate just for yourself, or a tiny, fruity layered pastry for two.

Small-batch baking is all about recipes that are developed to yield only a small amount. When I started experimenting with tiny batches of baked goods, I did so to minimize my use of flour, which was hard to find in the early stages of the pandemic. But beyond the pandemic, I realized it made sense for a lot of people, including me.

I love to bake, but I live alone. So, discovering the world of small-batch baking became a way for me to make things I wanted without being bogged down by leftovers. It's baking a plate of cookies to greet friends when they come over, or a few muffins when that's all you need for Sunday brunch. It's for the perfect tart to end a small, romantic dinner—or the indulgence of a one-bowl dessert just for you. Most of all, it's to bring home the joy of baking, when home is just one or two of you. Small batches whip up quickly, clean up quickly, and don't require hours in the oven. And, as someone who lives alone, it's nice knowing I can indulge my sweet tooth without the fear of having a ton of leftovers (for me to eat by myself) . . . ya know?!

That's where this book comes in. Here, you'll find 60 recipes for all types of small-batch treats: cakes, cookies, brownies, bars, pies, pastries, bread—even savory options. They're *all* included. These are basic, scaled-down recipes that every home baker should have in their arsenal, as well as innovative, fresh recipes that I hope you're excited to try.

So, whether you're watching what you eat, trying to eliminate food waste, or really just sick of having leftovers, this book is the perfect, easy, and delicious solution to your kitchen woes. I truly hope you enjoy these recipes as much as I've enjoyed creating them for you.

Let's bake something delicious, shall we?

Mike Johnson

ESSENTIAL BAKEWARE

It can be frustrating to have to go out and buy a new pan just for one recipe. Often, this specialty bakeware gets stored away collecting dust until *maybe* a year later, when you feel the urge to try that recipe again. And, that's a huge maybe . . . speaking from experience here. Most of the recipes in this book, however, can be made with standard bakeware and tools you likely already have on hand. To be sure, here's a brief list of what you will need:

DIGITAL KITCHEN SCALE: Smaller batches mean more room for error when it comes to measuring ingredients. I highly recommend using a scale and the metric measurements for the recipes in this book.

LOAF PANS: You'll need both the standard 9 x 5–inch (23 x 13–cm) loaf pan and the smaller 8 x 4–inch (20 x 10–cm) loaf pan.

CAKE PANS: You'll need 6 x 2–inch (15 x 5–cm) round pans, as well as an 8 x 8–inch (20 x 20–cm) square pan.

CUPCAKE/MUFFIN TIN: A 6-cup tin is all you need, but if you already have a 12-cup, that's fine; you'll just fill half the cups with batter and the other half with water to promote even baking.

RAMEKINS: These little dessert dishes usually come in a set of four, in various sizes. I recommend using the common 6-ounce (170-g) size. Also note: The ramekins will need to be either glass or ceramic and oven-safe.

SMALL SKILLET: Mini 6-inch (15-cm) cast iron or other oven-safe skillets are used for baking some dishes right in the pan. Skillet cookie or cobbler, anyone?

SMALL TART PANS: Tart pans that are 4.75 inches (12 cm) in size are the perfect individual serving size. You can also just use a standard 9-inch (23-cm) tart pan for the recipes that call for the small tart pans.

SHEET PAN: This common piece of bakeware comes in many sizes. The size of your sheet pan isn't important, just as long as you have one. It'll be used for things like cookies, pastries, and biscuits.

HAVE YOUR CAKE & EAT IT TOO

I love cake. Honestly, it's such a versatile dessert—it can be a layer cake, a sheet cake, a loaf, or even cupcakes; you can stack it, roll it, and even set it on fire (baked Alaska, anyone?). You can frost it, glaze it, or leave it plain. Serve cake warm, at room temperature, or chilled. I think you get the picture . . . the possibilities are endless. Whether you're celebrating something big, or it's just another Thursday, cake is always the answer. Due to the celebratory nature of cakes, however, one downside to most cake recipes is that they yield *a lot* of cake. And, that's great for large get-togethers or birthday parties, but not so great for when a random cake craving hits. Smaller cakes, like the ones in this chapter, are convenient for smaller celebrations or whenever you need a scaled-down cake.

In this chapter, you'll find my tried-and-true cake recipes. Like the Small-Batch Pumpkin Spice Cupcakes (page 36), which are packed full of perfectly spiced pumpkin flavor and topped with an insanely delicious Maple Cream Cheese Frosting. Or the Chocolate Peanut Butter Cake (page 21), which takes one of my favorite flavor combinations and packs it into an adorable mini layer cake. Or the Lemon Loaf Cake (page 25), which is really just a better version of the Starbucks lemon cake—try it for yourself and be amazed! When it comes to frosting, you'll find flavors that will please everyone: vanilla bean, chocolate fudge, brown butter cream cheese, and more. And, I totally encourage you to mix and match frostings as you see fit, because that's the beauty of cakes.

TIPS & TECHNIQUES

LINE THE CAKE PAN: What good is a delicious cake if it remains stuck in the pan? For smooth, easy removal, prep your pans properly with butter or nonstick cooking spray and parchment paper. For cupcakes, decorative preformed paper or foil liners are indispensable.

FOLDING: When incorporating dry ingredients into a batter, it is important not to overmix, which can cause tough cakes. The best way? Fold instead of stir. Here's how: Use the broad side of a silicone spatula, and drag it like an oar moving through water to suspend the dry ingredients in the batter. Turn the bowl regularly to make sure you bring the ingredients together evenly.

COOLING: Cakes and cupcakes cool faster and don't get soggy when set out on a rack. Leave them in the pans for 10 to 15 minutes before unmolding them, then place them on a rack to cool completely before frosting.

STORAGE: Store unfrosted cakes and cupcakes, well wrapped in plastic, at room temperature for 24 hours. Refrigerating cakes causes them to stale faster, so, for long-term storage, it's best to freeze them. Wrap the cake in plastic wrap and then heavy-duty foil to protect it from the cold, and let the cake thaw in the refrigerator before frosting it. To store frosted cakes, keep them at room temperature under a cake dome or large bowl, unless the recipe specifies refrigeration. For sliced cakes, press a piece of plastic wrap against the exposed surface to keep in moisture.

TOTAL TIME:
2 hours 30 minutes

MAKES: 4–6 slices

FOR THE RED VELVET CAKE

½ cup + 2 tbsp (75 g) cake flour

½ tbsp (3 g) unsweetened natural cocoa powder

¼ tsp baking soda

⅛ tsp fine sea salt

2 tbsp (28 g) unsalted butter, softened

¼ cup + 3 tbsp (88 g) granulated sugar

3 tbsp + 2 tsp (52 ml) canola oil

1 large egg, room temperature

1 tsp vanilla extract

¼ tsp distilled white vinegar or apple cider vinegar

½ tbsp (7 ml) red food coloring, see Ingredient Tip (page 14)

3 tbsp + 2 tsp (55 ml) buttermilk, room temperature

RED VELVET CAKE FOR TWO

To me, red velvet cake is the king of all cakes; the "I can't quite put my finger on the flavor" cake. It's a glorious combination of a mild chocolate flavor, tangy buttermilk, sweet vanilla, and butter. Its texture is worth writing home about, too. It's dense and soft, with a moist and velvety crumb (largely thanks to the cake flour). However, the absolute best part about red velvet cake is the frosting. I topped this cake with Ermine Buttercream, which pairs SO perfectly. If you've never heard of Ermine Buttercream, it's an old-school frosting, also called "boiled-milk frosting," that was the original icing for red velvet cake before cream cheese frosting took over in popularity. It's not too sweet, not too buttery, and not too heavy; think of a frosting as light as whipped cream but with way more character. Try it and thank me later!

Preheat the oven to 350°F (180°C). Grease one 6-inch (15-cm) cake pan, line it with parchment paper, then grease the parchment paper. Parchment paper helps the cake seamlessly release from the pan.

For the cake, in a medium bowl, whisk the flour, cocoa powder, baking soda, and salt together, then set it aside.

In a large bowl, using a handheld mixer, beat the butter and sugar together on medium-high speed until combined, about 1 minute. Scrape down the sides of the bowl with a rubber spatula as needed. Add the oil, egg, vanilla, vinegar, and food coloring, and beat the mixture on high for 2 minutes. Scrape down the sides and up the bottom of the bowl with a rubber spatula as needed.

With the mixer on low speed, add the dry ingredients in two to three additions, alternating with the buttermilk. The batter will be silky and slightly thick.

Transfer the batter to the prepared cake pan, and bake the cake for 30 to 32 minutes, or until the top of the cake springs back when gently touched and a toothpick inserted into the center comes out clean. If there are wet crumbs on the toothpick, bake the cake for longer. However, be careful not to overbake it, as the cake may dry out. Remove the cake from the oven and cool it completely in the pan, set on a wire rack. The cake must be completely cool before frosting.

(continued)

FOR THE ERMINE BUTTERCREAM

½ cup (100 g) granulated sugar

2½ tbsp (20 g) all-purpose flour

⅛ tsp fine sea salt

½ cup (120 ml) milk

½ cup (113 g) unsalted butter, softened

½ tsp vanilla bean paste

RED VELVET CAKE FOR TWO (CONTINUED)

To make the buttercream, begin by combining the sugar, flour, salt, and milk together in a small saucepan over medium heat. Bring the mixture to a boil, whisking continuously. Once boiling, continue to cook and whisk the mixture for about 3 minutes, or until the mixture becomes thick and glossy, like pudding.

Pour the mixture into a shallow, heat-safe bowl, and cover it with plastic wrap pressed directly onto the surface (to prevent a skin from forming). Let the mixture cool to room temperature, or refrigerate it for 15 to 20 minutes, until it's just cool to the touch but not solid.

In a stand mixer fitted with the paddle attachment, or in a large bowl using a handheld mixer, beat the butter on high speed until light and fluffy, about 1 minute. Turn the speed to medium-high, add the cooled milk mixture and vanilla bean paste, and beat the buttercream until it's smooth and light in texture and color. Use an offset spatula to cover the top of the cake completely with the frosting.

Cover leftover cake tightly and store it in the refrigerator for up to 5 days. Frosted cake or the unfrosted cake can be frozen for up to 3 months. Thaw the cake overnight in the refrigerator; bring it to room temperature before decorating or serving it.

VARIATION TIP: *Feel free to replace the Ermine Buttercream with a half-batch of the cream cheese frosting from the Mini Gingerbread Cake (page 26).*

INGREDIENT TIP: *For a vibrant red cake, use gel food coloring, which you can find online or at craft baking stores. Because it's more concentrated than liquid food coloring, you can use less of it—you'll only need ½ to 1 teaspoon—and still get brighter colors without thinning the cake batter or worrying about a weird food coloring taste.*

MAKE-AHEAD INSTRUCTIONS: *The cake can be baked, cooled, and covered tightly at room temperature overnight. Alternatively, you can wrap the cake tightly in plastic wrap, then again in aluminum foil, and freeze it for up to 3 months. Thaw the cake overnight in the refrigerator; bring it to room temperature before decorating or serving it.*

FOR THE CARROT CAKE CUPCAKES

½ cup + 2 tbsp (75 g) all-purpose flour

½ tsp baking powder

½ tsp baking soda

¼ tsp fine sea salt

½ tsp ground cinnamon

¼ tsp ground ginger

⅛ tsp ground nutmeg

⅛ tsp ground cloves

¼ cup (60 ml) canola oil

½ cup (110 g) dark brown sugar

1 large egg, room temperature

2 tbsp (30 g) sour cream, room temperature

½ tsp vanilla extract

½ cup (65 g) freshly grated carrots, approximately 1–2 carrots

FOR THE BROWN BUTTER CREAM CHEESE FROSTING

6 tbsp (85 g) unsalted butter, cubed

CARROT CAKE CUPCAKES

These Carrot Cake Cupcakes may not be the best way to get your daily serving of vegetables, but they're definitely the tastiest, especially when topped off with a generous swirl of Brown Butter Cream Cheese Frosting. They're soft, moist, and perfectly spiced. Not to mention, they're super easy to make, bake up in no time, and keep really well (if you even have leftovers). So, you can take them on picnics or lunches, or snack on them throughout the week!

Preheat the oven to 350°F (180°C). Line a 6-cup muffin pan with cupcake liners, then set it aside.

For the cupcakes, in a medium bowl, whisk together the flour, baking powder, baking soda, salt, cinnamon, ginger, nutmeg, and cloves, then set aside the mixture. In a separate medium bowl, whisk together the oil, brown sugar, egg, sour cream, and vanilla until combined; then whisk in the carrots. Pour the wet ingredients into the dry ingredients, and whisk until the ingredients are completely combined. The batter will be thick!

Spoon the batter into the prepared muffin pan, filling each liner until almost full; you'll use about 4 tablespoons (69 g) of batter per cup. Bake the cupcakes for 20 to 22 minutes, or until a toothpick inserted into the center comes out clean. Allow the cupcakes to cool completely before frosting them.

To make the frosting, begin by browning the butter. Place the butter in a light-colored skillet. (A light-colored skillet will help you determine when the butter begins browning.) Melt the butter over medium heat, stirring constantly. Once melted, the butter will start to foam. Keep stirring. After 5 to 8 minutes, the butter will begin browning; you'll notice lightly browned specks begin to form at the bottom of the pan, and you'll start to smell a nutty aroma. Once the butter is browned, immediately remove it from the heat, pour it into a medium heat-safe bowl, and refrigerate until it's solid, about 30 minutes. Alternatively, you can freeze the brown butter until solid, about 15 minutes.

(continued)

4 oz (113 g) cream cheese, softened

1½ cups (180 g) powdered sugar

½ tsp vanilla bean paste

⅛ tsp fine sea salt

¼ cup (30 g) chopped walnuts, optional

CARROT CAKE CUPCAKES (CONTINUED)

In the bowl of a stand mixer fitted with the paddle attachment, or using a handheld mixer, beat the solid brown butter on high speed until it's creamed. Add the cream cheese and beat on high speed until it's combined, smooth, and creamy, about 2 minutes. Add the powdered sugar, vanilla bean paste, and salt. Beat the mixture on low speed for 30 seconds, then switch to high speed and beat for 2 minutes, or until the frosting is smooth and fluffy and the ingredients are fully combined.

Frost the cooled cupcakes however you'd like and garnish with chopped walnuts, if using. I used a large French star piping tip (Ateco 866) for the cupcakes pictured. Store leftovers in an airtight container in the refrigerator for up to 5 days. Place them on the counter about an hour before you plan to serve them, so they can come to room temperature.

SUBSTITUTION TIP: *Sour cream gives these cupcakes their wonderfully moist texture and provides a hint of tanginess. Don't have any sour cream? Simply substitute an equal amount of Greek yogurt; just make sure it's plain or a compatible flavor!*

MAKE-AHEAD INSTRUCTIONS: *The cupcakes can be baked, cooled, covered tightly, and frozen for up to 3 months. Thaw them overnight in the refrigerator, and bring them to room temperature before frosting. Similarly, the frosting can also be made ahead and frozen in an airtight container for up to 3 months. Thaw it overnight in the refrigerator, bring it to room temperature, and mix it well before frosting the cupcakes.*

FOR THE FUNFETTI CAKE

1 cup + 2 tbsp (135 g) cake flour

½ cup + 1 tbsp (115 g) granulated sugar

½ tsp baking powder

½ tsp baking soda

⅛ tsp fine sea salt

6 tbsp (85 g) unsalted butter, softened

1 tsp vanilla bean paste

¼ cup + 2 tbsp (90 ml) milk, room temperature and divided

2 tbsp (30 g) sour cream, room temperature

1 large egg, room temperature

¼ cup (40 g) confetti sprinkles

LOAF PAN FUNFETTI SHEET CAKE

This Loaf Pan Funfetti Sheet Cake recipe uses the reverse creaming method. Instead of starting with creaming butter and sugar together, like traditional cake recipes, the reverse creaming method begins with the dry ingredients and ends with the eggs. This method produces a lighter and tighter crumb with more spring; the slices are tight like pound cake, but not dense in the slightest. The cake is velvety soft and almost tastes creamy, with the most delicious buttery vanilla flavor. It's topped with Vanilla Confetti Buttercream—a frosting made from butter, powdered sugar, and heavy cream and whipped until extra fluffy. Use this cake recipe as a mini birthday cake or for anytime you crave a simple, classic dessert!

Preheat the oven to 350°F (180°C). Line a 9 x 5–inch (23 x 13–cm) loaf pan with parchment paper, leaving an overhang on the two long sides. Lightly grease the parchment with butter or nonstick cooking spray, then set it aside.

For the cake, whisk the cake flour, sugar, baking powder, baking soda, and salt together in a large bowl. Add the butter, vanilla bean paste, and 3 tablespoons (45 ml) of the milk. Using a handheld mixer, beat on medium speed until the dry ingredients are moistened, about 1 minute. Stop the mixer and scrape down the sides and up the bottom of the bowl. The mixture will resemble a thick dough.

Whisk the remaining 3 tablespoons (45 ml) of milk, the sour cream, and egg together in a small measuring cup. With the mixer running on medium speed, add the egg mixture in three additions, mixing for about 15 seconds after each addition. Stop the mixer and scrape down the sides and up the bottom of the bowl, then mix for about 15 more seconds, until the batter is completely combined. Avoid overmixing; some small lumps are OK. Fold in the sprinkles until they are evenly dispersed.

Pour and spread the batter evenly into the prepared pan. Bake for 32 to 35 minutes, or until the cake is baked through. Begin checking for doneness at 30 minutes. To test for doneness, insert a toothpick into the center of the cake. If it comes out clean, it's done. Allow the cake to cool completely in the pan, set on a wire rack. The cake must be completely cool before frosting.

(continued)

FOR THE VANILLA CONFETTI BUTTERCREAM

6 tbsp (85 g) unsalted butter

1⅔ cups (200 g) powdered sugar

2 tbsp (30 ml) heavy cream

½ tsp vanilla bean paste

⅛ tsp fine sea salt

¼ cup (40 g) confetti sprinkles, plus more for garnish

While the cake cools, make the buttercream. With a handheld mixer, beat the butter on medium speed until creamy, about 1 minute. Add the powdered sugar, cream, vanilla bean paste, and salt. Beat on low speed for 30 seconds, then increase to medium-high speed and beat for 4 minutes. Add up to ¼ cup (30 g) more of powdered sugar if the frosting is too thin, or another tablespoon (15 ml) of heavy cream if the frosting is too thick. The frosting should be extra fluffy. Fold in the confetti sprinkles.

Spread the frosting in a thick layer on the cooled cake. I use and recommend an offset spatula. If desired, use a piping tip to pipe some frosting, then garnish the cake with additional sprinkles. Slice and serve. Cover leftover cake tightly, and store it in the refrigerator for up to 5 days.

MAKE-AHEAD INSTRUCTIONS: *The cake can be baked, cooled, and covered tightly at room temperature overnight. Alternatively, you can wrap the cake tightly in plastic wrap, then again in aluminum foil, and freeze it for up to 3 months.*

NOTE: *If you prefer a thinner layer of frosting (as pictured), halve the Vanilla Confetti Buttercream recipe.*

TOTAL TIME: 3 hours

MAKES: 6–8 slices

FOR THE CHOCOLATE PEANUT BUTTER CAKE

⅔ cup (147 g) light brown sugar

1 large egg, room temperature

⅓ cup (85 g) creamy peanut butter

⅓ cup + 1 tsp (85 ml) canola oil

⅓ cup + 1 tsp (85 ml) milk, room temperature

1 tsp vanilla extract

½ tsp fine sea salt

⅓ cup + 1 tbsp (30 g) unsweetened natural or Dutch-process cocoa powder

¾ cup (90 g) all-purpose flour

1 tsp baking powder

½ tsp baking soda

⅓ cup + 1 tsp (85 g) hot water

½ tsp espresso powder

FOR THE PEANUT BUTTER BUTTERCREAM

½ cup (113 g) unsalted butter, softened

⅓ cup (85 g) creamy peanut butter

2 cups (240 g) powdered sugar

1½–2 tbsp (22–30 ml) milk

⅛ tsp fine sea salt

CHOCOLATE PEANUT BUTTER CAKE

If you adore peanut butter and chocolate as much as I do, then you're going to LOVE this cake! It's easy to make, suuuuper moist, and it has such an intense chocolate peanut butter flavor; I mean that in the best way possible. The chocolate ganache drips really take it to the next level; it makes it taste just like a Reese's Peanut Butter Cup! You can use any brand of peanut butter in this recipe; just make sure you avoid the natural, unsweetened kind that has the oil on top and needs to be stirred—it'll make this cake extra oily.

Preheat the oven to 350°F (180°C). Grease two 6-inch (15-cm) cake pans, line them with parchment paper, then grease the parchment paper. Parchment paper helps the cakes seamlessly release from the pan.

For the cake, in a large bowl, whisk together the light brown sugar and egg until pale and foamy, about 1 minute. Add the peanut butter, oil, milk, vanilla, and salt, and whisk until well combined. Sift in the cocoa powder, and whisk it in until the batter is smooth.

Add the flour, baking powder, and baking soda, and whisk until combined and smooth. In a small cup, whisk together the hot water and espresso powder, then add that mixture into the batter, and stir until it's combined and smooth, about 1 minute.

Pour the batter into the prepared pans. Note that this recipe makes around 24 ounces (680 g) of batter; pour 12 ounces (340 g) into each cake pan. Bake the cakes for 30 to 33 minutes, or until the top of the cake bounces back when gently pressed and a toothpick inserted into the center of the cake comes out with only a few crumbs attached. Cool the cakes completely in the pans on a wire rack before frosting them.

For the buttercream, in the bowl of a stand mixer fitted with the paddle attachment, or in a large bowl with a handheld mixer, cream the butter and peanut butter together. Add the sugar, milk, and salt. Beat on low speed for 30 seconds, then increase to medium speed and beat for 2 minutes, or until the frosting is smooth and the ingredients are fully combined.

(continued)

6 oz (170 g) semisweet chocolate, finely chopped

½ cup (120 ml) heavy cream

INGREDIENT TIP: *The espresso powder in these cupcakes enhances the chocolate flavor. Unless you're extremely sensitive to coffee, you won't notice it at all. If you're worried about it, just omit the espresso powder altogether and only use hot water.*

MAKE-AHEAD INSTRUC-TIONS: *The cake can be baked, cooled, and covered tightly at room temperature overnight. Alternatively, you can wrap the cake tightly in plastic wrap, then again in aluminum foil, and freeze it for up to 3 months. Similarly, the frosting can also be made ahead of time and frozen in an airtight container for up to 3 months. Thaw the frosting overnight in the refrigerator, bring it to room temperature, and beat it well before frosting the cake.*

CHOCOLATE PEANUT BUTTER CAKE (CONTINUED)

To make the chocolate ganache, place the chocolate in a heat-safe bowl. In a saucepan over medium-high heat, warm the heavy cream until it just starts to simmer. Look for small bubbles forming around the edge and a soft simmer starting in the middle. Once it's reached this point, pour the cream into your bowl of chocolate, cover it with a tea towel, and allow it to sit for 30 to 60 seconds. Whisk it together until it's uniform in consistency and there are no bits of chocolate left. Cool the ganache at room temperature for 10 to 20 minutes.

Using a large, serrated knife, slice a thin layer off the tops of the cakes to create a flat surface, if needed. Place one cake layer on your cake stand or a serving plate, and evenly cover the top with a large dollop of frosting. Top with the second layer, placing it upside down (so the flat bottom of the cake is on top), and spread a thin layer of the frosting all over the top and sides for your crumb coat. Smooth the frosting with an offset spatula and bench scraper, and chill the cake for 10 to 20 minutes, or until the frosting has hardened slightly.

Pipe on additional Peanut Butter Buttercream over the crumb coat, and smooth the frosting with an offset spatula and bench scraper. Separate the remaining buttercream into two or three small bowls. Stir in various-sized dollops of ganache to each bowl, to achieve three different chocolate-colored frostings. Reserve the remaining ganache for the drip topping. Add random streaks of the various colored buttercreams to the outside of the cake. Smooth the frosting with a bench scraper, then chill the cake in the freezer for 10 minutes, or in the fridge for 20 minutes.

Complete a test drip on the cake to check the consistency of your ganache. If the test drip seems too thick, try heating up the ganache for 5 to 10 seconds in the microwave. If the mixture seems too thin and the ganache drips immediately to the bottom of the cake, allow it to cool a bit longer, then try another test drip. Add the drips using a small spoon or squeeze bottle; add the ganache to the edges of the cake and gently push it over the edge so that it falls, creating a drip. Continue adding drips around the outer edge until you've gone all the way around, then fill in the center with the remaining ganache and spread it evenly with an offset spatula. Pipe dollops of leftover buttercream around the edge of the cake on top.

Store the cake well-covered at room temperature for up to 3 days.

TOTAL TIME:
2 hours 30 minutes

MAKES: 8–10 slices

FOR THE LEMON CAKE

¾ cup (90 g) all-purpose flour

¾ cup (90 g) cake flour

½ tsp baking powder

¼ tsp baking soda

½ tsp fine sea salt

1 cup (200 g) granulated sugar

2 tbsp (10 g) lemon zest, approximately 2 medium lemons

3 large eggs, room temperature

⅓ cup (80 g) sour cream, room temperature

¼ cup (57 g) unsalted butter, melted

¼ cup (60 ml) canola oil

2 tsp (10 ml) lemon extract

2 tbsp (30 ml) freshly squeezed lemon juice

FOR THE LEMON GLAZE

1 cup (120 g) powdered sugar

2 tbsp (30 ml) freshly squeezed lemon juice

¼ tsp lemon extract

LEMON LOAF CAKE

*Have you ever tried the lemon loaf from Starbucks? If you ask me, it's the best thing in their bakery case. It's bursting with bright and sunny lemon flavor, and it's blanketed with the perfect layer of sweet lemon glaze. It also has the most irresistible tender, pillowy texture. I was instantly smitten the first time I tried it, and knew I had to re-create it at home. And, after a few rounds of experimenting—and lots of delicious taste-testing—I can confidently say this version is even **better** than the one from Starbucks. Best of all, you can have a slice whenever you please. A word of advice: Make sure you use room temperature ingredients, because it really does make a difference. Having the ingredients at room temperature helps the batter mix together more evenly and results in a lighter, fluffier cake. So, don't skip over that step!*

Preheat the oven to 350°F (180°C), and line an 8 x 4–inch (20 x 10–cm) loaf pan with parchment paper, with an overhang on the two long sides. Coat the paper with nonstick cooking spray, then set aside the pan.

For the cake, in a medium bowl, whisk together the all-purpose flour, cake flour, baking powder, baking soda, and salt, then set the bowl aside. Add the granulated sugar to a large bowl and, using your fingers, rub the lemon zest into the sugar until it's well combined and fragrant. Add the eggs, sour cream, butter, oil, lemon extract, and lemon juice, and whisk until the sugar is dissolved and no lumps from the sour cream remain, 2 to 3 minutes.

Add the flour mixture and whisk until smooth, about 1 minute. Transfer the batter to the prepared pan and smooth the top with a spatula. Bake until the cake is lightly browned and a toothpick inserted into the center comes out clean, 50 to 60 minutes. Let the cake cool for 15 minutes in the pan. Remove the cake from the pan using the parchment paper sling, place it on a wire rack, and let it cool completely, 45 minutes to 1 hour.

For the glaze, in a small bowl, whisk together the sugar, lemon juice, and lemon extract until the mixture is smooth and creamy. Spread the glaze evenly over the top of the cake, letting some of it drip down the sides. Let the cake sit until the icing is set, about 30 minutes. Store leftover cake, wrapped tightly in plastic wrap, at room temperature for up to 4 days.

FOR THE GINGERBREAD CAKE

1¾ cup (220 g) all-purpose flour

1 tsp baking soda

2 tsp (4 g) ground cinnamon

1½ tsp (3 g) ground ginger

¼ tsp ground cloves

¼ tsp ground nutmeg

⅛ tsp ground allspice

½ tsp fine sea salt

⅓ cup + 2 tbsp (100 g) dark brown sugar

¼ cup + 1 tbsp (60 g) granulated sugar

¼ cup + 2 tsp (70 ml) canola oil

1 large egg, room temperature

⅓ cup + 2 tbsp (150 g) molasses

1 tsp vanilla extract

⅔ cup (160 ml) hot water

FOR THE CREAM CHEESE FROSTING

7 oz (198 g) cream cheese, softened

⅓ cup (76 g) unsalted butter, softened

1 tsp vanilla bean paste

⅛ tsp fine sea salt

2⅓ cups (280 g) powdered sugar

MINI GINGERBREAD CAKE

It's safe to say my sweet tooth is in full gear when the holidays roll around. And, this gingerbread cake is usually near the top of my list. The combination of ginger, cinnamon, nutmeg, cloves, and allspice will leave you salivating! Not to mention, it's all topped off with a Cream Cheese Frosting that makes everything taste better. This stuff is what Christmas dreams are made of!

Preheat the oven to 350°F (180°C). Grease two 6-inch (15-cm) cake pans, line them with parchment paper, then grease the parchment paper. Parchment paper helps the cakes seamlessly release from the pan.

For the cake, in a medium bowl, whisk together the flour, baking soda, cinnamon, ginger, cloves, nutmeg, allspice, and salt, then set aside the bowl. In a large bowl, whisk together the dark brown sugar, granulated sugar, oil, and egg until well combined; then whisk in the molasses. Add the vanilla and hot water, then whisk together until completely combined; do this carefully, as the water will splash around at first! Pour the dry ingredients into the wet ingredients, and whisk until the ingredients are completely combined. The batter will be fairly thin!

Pour the batter into the prepared pans. Note that this recipe makes around 28½ ounces (810 g) of batter; pour 14 ounces (405 g) into each cake pan. Bake the cakes for 28 to 32 minutes, or until the top of the cake bounces back when gently pressed and a toothpick inserted into the center of the cake comes out with only a few crumbs attached. Cool the cakes for 15 minutes in the pans, then transfer them to a wire rack to cool completely. The cakes must be completely cool before frosting and assembling.

To make the frosting, place the cream cheese and butter in the bowl of a stand mixer fitted with the paddle attachment, or in a large bowl using a handheld mixer, and cream on medium-high speed until combined and smooth, 2 to 3 minutes. Add the vanilla bean paste and salt, and beat until combined. Add the sugar and beat on low speed for 30 seconds, then switch to high speed, and beat for 2 minutes, or until the frosting is smooth and the sugar is fully combined.

(continued)

MINI GINGERBREAD CAKE (CONTINUED)

Using a large, serrated knife, slice a thin layer off the tops of the cakes to create a flat surface, if needed. Place one cake layer on your cake stand or serving plate, and evenly cover the top with a large dollop of frosting. Top with the second layer, placing it upside down (so the flat bottom of the cake is on top), and spread a thin layer of the frosting all over the top and sides for your crumb coat. Smooth the frosting with an offset spatula and bench scraper. Chill the cake for 10 to 20 minutes, or until the frosting has hardened slightly.

Pipe on additional frosting over the crumb coat, and smooth the frosting with an offset spatula and bench scraper. Pipe additional decorations on the sides and top of the cake with leftover frosting, if desired. Store the cake well-covered at room temperature for up to 3 days.

MAKE-AHEAD INSTRUCTIONS: *The cake can be baked, cooled, and covered tightly at room temperature overnight. Alternatively, you can wrap the cake tightly in plastic wrap, then again in aluminum foil, and freeze it for up to 3 months. Similarly, the frosting can also be made ahead of time and frozen in an airtight container for up to 3 months. Thaw the frosting overnight in the refrigerator, bring it to room temperature, and beat it well before frosting the cake.*

FOR THE CHOCOLATE CUPCAKES

½ cup (60 g) all-purpose flour

2 tbsp (10 g) unsweetened natural cocoa powder

¼ tsp baking soda

¼ tsp fine sea salt

1 oz (28 g) 70% cacao dark chocolate, finely chopped

2 tbsp (28 g) unsalted butter

½ cup (100 g) granulated sugar

1 large egg, room temperature

1 tsp vanilla extract

¼ cup (60 g) sour cream, room temperature

¼ cup (60 ml) hot water

⅛ tsp espresso powder, see Ingredient Tip (page 31)

DEATH BY CHOCOLATE CUPCAKES

What we have here are rich, moist chocolate cupcakes, smothered in a bold and glorious Chocolate Fudge Buttercream. They have a fantastic contrast of textures and are so perfectly chocolaty for those times when you desperately need a chocolate fix. Made with melted chocolate, cocoa powder, and espresso powder, the chocolate flavor in these cupcakes is intense. Death doesn't appeal to me much, but if you gotta go . . . why not by chocolate!?

Preheat the oven to 350°F (180°C). Line a 6-cup muffin pan with cupcake liners, then set it aside.

For the cupcakes, in a small bowl, whisk together the flour, cocoa powder, baking soda, and salt, then set aside the bowl. Place the chocolate and butter in a large heat-safe bowl, and set it over a pan of gently simmering water to create a double boiler; mix until the ingredients are completely smooth and melted. Alternatively, melt the chocolate and butter in the microwave, heating them in 30-second intervals and mixing thoroughly between each interval. Once the chocolate is fully melted, remove the bowl from the heat, and stir in the sugar.

Add the egg, vanilla, and sour cream, and whisk until the mixture is well combined, scraping down the sides and up the bottom of the bowl as needed. Add in the dry ingredients and whisk until they are just incorporated. In a small cup, whisk together the hot water and espresso powder, then add that mixture into the batter and whisk until completely combined and smooth, about 1 minute. (Do this carefully as the water will splash around at first!)

Spoon the batter into the prepared pan, filling each liner until almost full; you'll use about 4 tablespoons (62 g) of batter per cup. Bake the cupcakes for 18 to 20 minutes, or until a toothpick inserted into the center comes out relatively clean with a few moist crumbs. Allow the cupcakes to cool completely before frosting them.

(continued)

**FOR THE CHOCOLATE FUDGE
BUTTERCREAM**

1½ oz (42 g) 70% cacao dark
chocolate, finely chopped

6 tbsp (85 g) unsalted butter,
softened

1 cup (120 g) powdered sugar

½ tsp vanilla extract

1 tbsp (15 ml) milk

⅛ tsp fine sea salt

Chocolate syrup, optional

DEATH BY CHOCOLATE CUPCAKES (CONTINUED)

To make the buttercream, begin by melting the chocolate. Place the chopped chocolate in a heat-safe bowl and set it over a pan of gently simmering water to create a double boiler; stir until the chocolate is completely smooth and melted. Alternatively, melt the chocolate in the microwave, heating it in 30-second intervals and mixing thoroughly between each interval. Once the chocolate is fully melted, remove the bowl from the heat and set it aside to cool slightly.

In the bowl of a stand mixer fitted with the paddle attachment, or in a large bowl with a handheld mixer, beat the butter on medium speed until creamy, about 1 minute. Add the sugar, vanilla, milk, and salt. Beat on low speed for 30 seconds, then increase speed to medium-high, and beat for 2 full minutes. Add the melted chocolate, and beat the mixture on high speed for another 1 to 2 minutes, until the frosting is fluffy and the ingredients are completely combined. Add more powdered sugar if the frosting is too thin, more milk if the frosting is too thick, or an extra pinch of salt if the frosting is too sweet. The frosting should be soft and creamy, but not runny.

Frost the cooled cupcakes however you'd like and garnish them with the chocolate syrup, if using. I used a large closed star piping tip (Wilton 2D) for the cupcakes pictured. Store leftovers in an airtight container in the refrigerator for up to 4 days. Place the cupcakes on the counter about an hour before you plan to serve them, so they can come to room temperature.

INGREDIENT TIP: *The espresso powder in these cupcakes enhances the chocolate flavor. Unless you're extremely sensitive to coffee, you won't notice it at all. If you're worried about it, just omit the espresso powder altogether and only use hot water.*

MAKE-AHEAD INSTRUCTIONS: *The cupcakes can be baked, cooled, covered tightly, and frozen for up to 3 months. Thaw them overnight in the refrigerator, and bring them to room temperature before frosting. Similarly, the frosting can also be made ahead of time and frozen in an airtight container for up to 3 months. Thaw it overnight in the refrigerator, bring it to room temperature, and beat it well before frosting the cupcakes.*

MAKES: 8 slices

FOR THE APPLE CAKE

½ cup (110 g) light brown sugar

1 tbsp + 2 tsp (26 ml) vegetable oil

1 tbsp + 1 tsp (20 g) applesauce

⅓ cup (80 ml) milk

½ tsp vanilla extract

¾ cup + 2 tbsp (110 g) all-purpose flour

½ tsp ground cinnamon

¼ tsp baking soda

⅛ tsp fine sea salt

½ cup (90 g) grated apples

FOR THE STREUSEL TOPPING

¼ cup (55 g) dark brown sugar

¼ cup (30 g) all-purpose flour

¼ tsp ground cinnamon

⅛ tsp fine sea salt

2 tbsp (28 g) unsalted butter, softened

FOR THE VANILLA GLAZE

¼ cup (30 g) powdered sugar

½ tbsp (7 ml) milk

¼ tsp vanilla bean paste (or vanilla extract)

SMALL-BATCH APPLE CINNAMON COFFEE CAKE

If you're craving a rich, perfectly spiced apple cake and love a good streusel topping, then this cake was made for you. It's one of the moistest cakes I have ever made, and it tastes amazing. Not only is this apple streusel snack cake ridiculously delicious, but it's also ridiculously easy to make. It's one bowl—well, excluding the streusel and glaze—so if you can mix, stir, and pour, you can make this cake!

Preheat the oven to 350°F (180°C), and grease an 8 x 4–inch (20 x 10–cm) loaf pan or line it with parchment paper. Set aside the pan.

For the cake, in a large bowl, whisk together the sugar, oil, and applesauce until combined. Add the milk and vanilla, and whisk again until the mixture is well combined.

Using a silicone spatula, stir in the flour, cinnamon, baking soda, and salt until just combined. Add the apples and stir until evenly incorporated. Transfer the batter to the prepared pan and set it aside.

For the streusel, in a small bowl, whisk together the sugar, flour, cinnamon, and salt. Add the butter and, using a fork, mix until the ingredients are well combined and crumbles form. Sprinkle the streusel on top of the batter in an even layer.

Bake the cake for 33 to 35 minutes, or until a toothpick inserted into the center comes out clean and relatively crumb-free. Remove the cake from the oven, and let it cool while you make the vanilla glaze.

To make the glaze, add the sugar, milk, and vanilla bean paste to a small bowl, and whisk until the mixture is well combined and smooth. If the icing is too thin, add a little more powdered sugar; if it's too thick, add more milk. Drizzle the glaze over the warm cake!

This coffee cake is best served the same day it is prepared, but it can be covered tightly and stored at room temperature or in the refrigerator for 2 to 3 days!

TOTAL TIME:
1 hour 30 minutes

MAKES: 6 cupcakes

FOR THE VANILLA BEAN CUPCAKES

¾ cup + 2 tsp (95 g) cake flour

1 tsp baking powder

¼ tsp fine sea salt

¼ cup (57 g) unsalted butter, softened

½ cup (100 g) granulated sugar

1 large egg, room temperature

3 tbsp (45 g) sour cream, room temperature

1 tsp vanilla extract

Seeds scraped from ½ of a vanilla bean or ½ tsp vanilla bean paste

⅓ cup (80 ml) milk

FOR THE VANILLA BEAN BUTTERCREAM

½ cup (113 g) unsalted butter

2 cups (240 g) powdered sugar

2 tbsp (30 ml) heavy cream

1 tsp vanilla extract

Seeds scraped from ½ of a vanilla bean or ½ tsp vanilla bean paste

⅛ tsp fine sea salt

VANILLA BEAN CUPCAKES

When it comes to cupcakes, there is one very important question to answer: Are you Team Chocolate or Team Vanilla? If you're Team Chocolate, then you'll want to take a look at page 29 . . . but for all my vanilla lovers, this is about to become your go-to recipe: A moist vanilla bean cake base, topped with swirls of fluffy vanilla bean frosting.

Preheat the oven to 350°F (180°C). Line a 6-cup muffin pan with cupcake liners, then set it aside.

For the cupcakes, in a medium bowl, whisk together the flour, baking powder, and salt, then set aside the mixture. In a separate medium bowl, using a handheld mixer, beat the butter on high speed until it's smooth and creamy, about 1 minute. Add the sugar and beat on high speed for 2 minutes, until it's creamed together. Scrape down the sides and up the bottom of the bowl with a rubber spatula as needed.

Add the egg, sour cream, vanilla extract, and vanilla bean seeds. Beat on medium-high speed until the ingredients are combined, scraping down the sides and up the bottom of the bowl as needed. With the mixer on low speed, add the dry ingredients until they are just incorporated. With the mixer still running on low, slowly pour in the milk until it's combined.

Spoon the batter into the prepared pan, filling each liner until almost full; you'll use about 4 tablespoons (60 g) of batter per cup. Bake the cupcakes for 20 to 22 minutes, or until a toothpick inserted into the center comes out relatively clean with a few moist crumbs. Allow the cupcakes to cool completely before frosting them.

For the buttercream, in the bowl of a stand mixer fitted with the paddle attachment, or in a large bowl with a handheld mixer, beat the butter on medium speed until creamy, about 1 minute. Add the sugar, cream, vanilla extract, vanilla bean seeds, and salt. Beat on low speed for 30 seconds, then increase to medium-high and beat for 2 full minutes, or until the mixture is smooth and the ingredients are fully combined.

Frost the cooled cupcakes however you'd like. I used a large open star piping tip (Wilton 1M) for the cupcakes pictured. Store leftovers in an airtight container in the refrigerator for up to 4 days. Place cupcakes on the counter about an hour before you plan to serve them, so they can come to room temperature.

MAKE-AHEAD INSTRUCTIONS: *The cupcakes can be baked, cooled, covered tightly, and frozen for up to 3 months. Thaw them overnight in the refrigerator, and bring them to room temperature before frosting. Similarly, the frosting can also be made ahead of time and frozen in an airtight container for up to 3 months. Thaw the frosting overnight in the refrigerator, bring it to room temperature, and beat it well before frosting the cupcakes.*

MAKES: 4 cupcakes

FOR THE PUMPKIN SPICE CUPCAKES

½ cup (60 g) all-purpose flour

½ tsp baking powder

¼ tsp baking soda

⅛ tsp fine sea salt

½ tsp pumpkin pie spice

2½ tbsp (38 ml) canola oil

¼ cup (55 g) light brown sugar

2 tbsp (25 g) granulated sugar

¼ cup + 2½ tbsp (100 g) pumpkin puree, see Ingredient Tips (page 38)

½ tsp vanilla extract

FOR THE MAPLE CREAM CHEESE FROSTING

2½ oz (71 g) cream cheese, softened

2 tbsp (28 g) unsalted butter, softened

1 cup + 2 tbsp (135 g) powdered sugar

⅛ tsp fine sea salt

1 tbsp (20 g) pure maple syrup, see Ingredient Tips (page 38)

SMALL-BATCH PUMPKIN SPICE CUPCAKES

There are just days in life when you want (need?) something sweet, but also want to keep it simple. Not to mention, the prospect of a dozen-plus cupcakes leftover on your counter is a recipe for regret and bad feelings. That's where these Small-Batch Pumpkin Spice Cupcakes come in! Sweet and full of spice, these cupcakes are moist, delicious, and topped with generous swirls of Maple Cream Cheese Frosting: the perfect treat for the fall season!

Preheat the oven to 350°F (180°C). Line a 6-cup muffin pan with 4 cupcake liners, then set aside the pan.

For the cupcakes, in a small bowl, whisk together the flour, baking powder, baking soda, salt, and pumpkin pie spice, then set aside the bowl.

In a medium bowl, whisk together the oil, brown sugar, granulated sugar, pumpkin puree, and vanilla until combined. Add the dry ingredients and whisk until they are completely combined. The batter will be slightly thick.

Spoon the batter into the prepared pan, filling each liner about two-thirds full; you'll use about 3 tablespoons (65 g) of batter per cup. Bake the cupcakes for 18 to 20 minutes, or until a toothpick inserted into the center comes out clean. Allow the cupcakes to cool completely before frosting them.

For the frosting, in the bowl of a stand mixer fitted with the paddle attachment, or in a medium bowl using a handheld mixer, beat the cream cheese and butter on high speed until creamed and combined, about 2 minutes. Add the sugar and salt, and beat the mixture on low speed for 30 seconds, then switch to high speed and beat for 1 minute. Add the maple syrup, and beat on medium-high speed until it's combined and the frosting is fluffy, 2 to 3 minutes.

(continued)

SMALL-BATCH PUMPKIN SPICE CUPCAKES (CONTINUED)

Frost the cooled cupcakes however you'd like. I used a large round piping tip (Wilton 1A) for the cupcakes pictured.

Store leftovers in an airtight container in the refrigerator for up to 4 days. Place them on the counter about an hour before you plan to serve them, so they can come to room temperature.

INGREDIENT TIPS: *Leftover pumpkin puree can be transferred to an airtight container and refrigerated for 1 week, or frozen for up to 3 months.*

Be sure to use pure maple syrup and not pancake/table syrup. If you're unsure, try reading the ingredients label. The number one ingredient in pancake/table syrup is usually corn syrup, followed by high-fructose corn syrup. True maple syrup will have no list and will simply say "organic maple syrup" or "pure maple syrup."

MAKE-AHEAD INSTRUCTIONS: *The cupcakes can be baked, cooled, covered tightly, and frozen for up to 3 months. Thaw them overnight in the refrigerator, and bring them to room temperature before frosting. Similarly, the frosting can also be made ahead of time and frozen in an airtight container for up to 3 months. Thaw it overnight in the refrigerator, bring it to room temperature, and beat it well before frosting the cupcakes.*

TOTAL TIME: 3 hours

MAKES: 6 slices

FOR THE CHOCOLATE PEPPERMINT CAKE

½ cup (113 g) unsalted butter, softened

¾ cup (150 g) granulated sugar

2 large eggs, room temperature

1 tsp vanilla extract

½ tsp peppermint extract

1 cup (120 g) all-purpose flour

⅓ cup + 1 tbsp (30 g) unsweetened natural or Dutch-process cocoa powder

¼ tsp baking powder

¼ tsp baking soda

½ tsp fine sea salt

½ cup (120 ml) buttermilk, room temperature

CHOCOLATE PEPPERMINT CAKE

This recipe involves two of my all-time favorite flavors of Christmas: chocolate and peppermint. It's basically peppermint bark in cake form . . . so, like, it's perfect. It has moist chocolate cake layers with a hint of peppermint, all topped with a white chocolate peppermint frosting. Need I say more?! I'm not dreaming of a white Christmas . . . I'm dreaming about making this cake again!

Preheat the oven to 350°F (180°C). Grease two 6-inch (15-cm) cake pans, line them with parchment paper, then grease the parchment paper. Parchment paper helps the cakes seamlessly release from the pan.

For the cake, in a large bowl using a handheld mixer, beat the butter on high speed until it's smooth and creamy, about 1 minute. Add the sugar and beat on high speed for 2 minutes, or until it's creamed together. Scrape down the sides and up the bottom of the bowl with a rubber spatula as needed. Add the eggs, vanilla, and peppermint extract, and beat until combined.

In a medium bowl, combine the flour, cocoa powder, baking powder, baking soda, and salt, and whisk until combined. With the mixer on low speed, add the dry ingredients in two to three additions, alternating with the buttermilk. The batter will be thick.

Pour the batter into the prepared pans and smooth out the top. Note that this recipe makes around 23 ounces (645 g) of batter; pour 11.5 ounces (323 g) into each cake pan. Bake the cakes for 25 to 27 minutes, or until the top of the cake bounces back when gently pressed and a toothpick inserted into the center of the cake comes out with a few crumbs attached. Cool the cakes completely in the pans on a wire rack before frosting them.

(continued)

FOR THE WHITE CHOCOLATE PEPPERMINT BUTTERCREAM

6 oz (170 g) white chocolate, finely chopped

1 cup (227 g) unsalted butter, room temperature

2¼ cups (270 g) powdered sugar

¼ cup (60 ml) heavy cream, room temperature

1 tsp vanilla extract

½ tsp peppermint extract

⅛ tsp fine sea salt

Crushed peppermints, for garnish

CHOCOLATE PEPPERMINT CAKE (CONTINUED)

To make the buttercream, begin by melting the chocolate. Place it in a heat-safe bowl and set it over a pan of gently simmering water to create a double boiler; stir until the chocolate is completely smooth and melted. Alternatively, melt the chocolate in the microwave, heating it in 30-second intervals and mixing thoroughly between each interval. Once the chocolate is fully melted, remove the bowl from the heat and set it aside to cool the chocolate slightly, about 10 minutes.

In the bowl of a stand mixer fitted with the paddle attachment, or in a large bowl using a handheld mixer, beat the butter on high speed until it's completely smooth and creamy, 2 to 3 minutes. Switch to medium-high speed and beat in the sugar, cream, vanilla, peppermint extract, and salt. Once combined, switch to low speed and slowly pour the slightly cooled white chocolate in, with the mixer running. Beat until the ingredients are smooth and fully combined.

Using a large, serrated knife, slice a thin layer off the tops of the cakes to create a flat surface, if needed. Place one cake layer on your cake stand or serving plate, and evenly cover the top with a large dollop of frosting. Top with the second layer, placing it upside down (so the flat bottom of the cake is on top), and spread a thin layer of the frosting all over the top and sides for your crumb coat. Smooth the frosting with an offset spatula and bench scraper and chill the cake until the frosting has hardened slightly, 10 to 20 minutes.

Pipe on the rest of the buttercream over the crumb coat, and smooth it with an offset spatula and bench scraper. Pipe dollops of leftover buttercream around the edge of the cake, and sprinkle it with the peppermints.

Store the cake in an airtight container in the fridge for up to 4 days.

CRAZY FOR COOKIES

I've never met someone who dislikes cookies. And, honestly, what's not to like? These little circular treats can be soft, chewy, or crispy; chocolaty, citrusy, or spicy—the options are endless! Plus, they range from super simple to extremely complicated (I'm looking at you, macarons). Sometimes all you want is one outrageously delicious cookie (OK, maybe three if they're small or really good), but most cookie recipes yield a dozen or more, which isn't ideal if you're easily tempted by leftovers. That's where this chapter comes into play . . .

In this chapter, you'll find my go-to cookie recipes for when I want an easy sweet treat. There's the Brown Butter Bourbon Snickerdoodles (page 53), which have become one of my favorites and is the recipe I always make when I have friends coming over. The Small-Batch Black-and-White Cookies (page 57) are a staple here in New York City and surprisingly easy to make. Whether you're just starting out or you're a cookie connoisseur, there's sure to be a recipe in this chapter that you'll enjoy!

TIPS & TECHNIQUES

CREAMING BUTTER AND SUGAR: Properly creamed butter and sugar is the key to cookies with the best texture—when they call for softened butter, that is. Creaming whips air into the mixture, creating a light, fluffy cookie with a nice bit of chew. To start, you need butter at the right temperature: Butter is softened when you press your finger into the butter and it gives but mostly holds its shape.

ELECTRIC MIXERS: You can make the recipes in this chapter with a whisk and some elbow grease, but I call for a handheld mixer for some because, for the best texture, they require mixing times of 2 minutes or more. If you don't have a mixer, you can purchase a quality one for less than $30—or you can mix these recipes by hand. Electric mixers are (obviously) more powerful than an arm, so you may need to whisk longer than the recommended time to achieve the proper texture.

TESTING FOR DONENESS: Rely on visual cues like browning and/or set edges. Cookies have more wiggle room than most baked goods because underdone versus overdone is largely a matter of opinion. Each recipe will include any relevant visual cues to look for, but if you have strong feelings on the subject, trust your instincts!

STORAGE: Unless otherwise noted, these recipes can be stored at room temperature in an airtight container and will generally stay fresh for up to 5 days. Unbaked dough can be kept in the refrigerator—wrapped in plastic wrap—for up to 24 hours. Cookies also freeze rather well, both baked and raw.

To freeze cookie dough, prepare the cookies up to the point when you'd put them in the oven, and stick them in the freezer instead. Once frozen solid, you can store the dough balls in a freezer bag without them sticking together. Bake frozen cookies at the recommended temperature for just a couple minutes longer than the recipe calls for. To freeze baked cookies, freeze them in an airtight container until you're ready to eat them. Thaw them on a cooling rack when you are ready to eat them! Frozen dough and baked goods are best if used and eaten within 3 months.

TOTAL TIME: 1 hour

MAKES: 6 cookies

¼ cup (57 g) unsalted butter, softened

¼ cup (55 g) light brown sugar

1 tbsp (12 g) granulated sugar

1 large egg yolk, room temperature

½ tsp vanilla extract

½ cup + 2 tbsp (75 g) all-purpose flour

¼ tsp baking soda

¼ tsp fine sea salt

½ cup (85 g) chocolate chips

6 soft caramels, see Ingredient Tip

Flaky sea salt, optional

CARAMEL-STUFFED CHOCOLATE CHIP COOKIES

These are the perfect cookies. They're big, but not ridiculously so, packed with just the right amount of chocolate and caramel, and have the ideal texture: a little crisp at the edges, soft and chewy in the center. And, thanks to the egg yolk in the batter, they brown beautifully. These are definitely Instagram-worthy cookies that everyone will be drooling over.

Line a baking sheet with parchment paper, and set aside the pan.

In a medium bowl using a handheld mixer, beat the butter, brown sugar, and granulated sugar together on medium speed until the mixture is light and fluffy, about 2 minutes. Add the egg yolk and vanilla and beat until the ingredients are incorporated. Add in the flour, baking soda, and salt and mix on low speed until they are just combined. Stir in the chocolate chips until they are evenly incorporated.

Using a large (3-tablespoon [42-g]) spring-loaded cookie scoop, portion out the dough into six rounded balls. Flatten each dough ball into a flat circle, place a caramel in the center of the flattened dough, and then form the dough into a ball around the caramel, making sure it's completely sealed inside.

Place the cookie dough balls onto the prepared baking sheet 2 inches (5 cm) apart and refrigerate them uncovered for 15 minutes. While the cookie dough chills, preheat the oven to 375°F (190°C). Bake the dough balls for 9 to 10 minutes, or until the edges are golden brown and the tops are just set.

Remove the cookies from the oven, sprinkle them with the flaky salt, if using, and allow them to cool completely on the baking sheet. Store leftovers in an airtight container for up to 4 days. I love popping them in the microwave for about 10 seconds to warm them up and make them gooey.

VARIATION TIP: *Feel free to omit the caramels completely for an easy small-batch chocolate chip cookie recipe! Once you portion out the six dough balls, simply chill the dough in the fridge for fifteen minutes before baking it, as instructed in the recipe.*

INGREDIENT TIP: *I have tested this recipe with several brands of caramel candy and they all turned out delicious with slight differences. Softer old-fashioned caramels, such as Werther's®, will melt more into the cookie as it bakes; harder Kraft caramels will retain their shape and give the cookies a slight domed top.*

MAKES: 8 cookies

½ cup (100 g) granulated sugar

1 tbsp (5 g) lemon zest, approximately 1 medium lemon

¼ cup (57 g) unsalted butter, softened

2 tbsp (30 ml) freshly squeezed lemon juice

2 tbsp (30 g) applesauce

½ tsp vanilla extract

1 cup + 2 tsp (125 g) all-purpose flour

⅛ tsp fine sea salt

½ tsp baking soda

Sparkling sugar, for rolling, optional

LEMON SUGAR COOKIES

Buttery, chewy, and with the tart bite of lemon, these cookies are addictive. I could eat a dozen of them easily, which is exactly why I love this small-batch version. I happily devour my self-allotted two cookies and my work is done; my sweet tooth craving is fully satisfied, at least until the remaining cookies start calling my name!

Line a baking sheet with parchment paper, and set aside the pan.

In a medium bowl, combine the granulated sugar and lemon zest. Using your fingers, rub the zest into the sugar until it's well combined and fragrant. Add the butter. Using a handheld mixer, beat the butter and sugar together until they are combined and fluffy, about 2 minutes. Add the lemon juice, applesauce, and vanilla, and beat until combined. Don't worry if the mixture looks a little curdled!

Add the flour, salt, and baking soda, and stir the mixture with a rubber spatula until the ingredients are well combined. Using a large (3-tablespoon [42-g]) spring-loaded cookie scoop, portion out the dough into eight rounded dough balls and roll them in the sparkling sugar, if using. Place the cookie dough balls onto the baking sheet 2 inches (5 cm) apart, cover them loosely with plastic wrap, and place the pan in the refrigerator to chill the dough for 30 minutes. While the cookie dough chills, preheat the oven to 350°F (180°C).

Bake the dough balls for 12 to 14 minutes, or until the edges and the tops are just set. Allow the cookies to cool completely on the baking sheet. Store leftovers in an airtight container for up to 4 days.

TOTAL TIME: 40 minutes

MAKES: 1 (6-inch [15-cm]) skillet cookie

¼ cup (57 g) unsalted butter, melted

2½ tbsp (30 g) granulated sugar

¼ cup (55 g) dark brown sugar

1 large egg yolk

1 tsp vanilla extract

½ cup (60 g) all-purpose flour

¼ tsp baking soda

¼ tsp fine sea salt

¼ cup (44 g) chocolate chips

¼ cup (33 g) chopped pecans

Flaky sea salt, optional

Vanilla ice cream, optional

Chocolate syrup, optional

CHOCOLATE PECAN SKILLET COOKIE FOR TWO

This right here is complete cookie heaven; it's a soft and chewy skillet cookie loaded with chocolate chips and pecans, baked in a cast iron pan, and served warm with ice cream on top. The lack of rolling and chilling the dough makes this a quick and easy dessert that's sure to be a hit. With an ooey-gooey center and crispy edges, this cookie is absolutely delicious! It's a perfectly indulgent dessert that requires two spoons, one for you and your best other—or one for each hand!

Preheat the oven to 350°F (180°C). Lightly grease a 6-inch (15-cm) oven-safe skillet, and set it aside.

In a medium bowl, whisk together the butter, granulated sugar, and brown sugar until combined, about 1 minute. Beat in the egg yolk and vanilla, scraping down the sides and bottom of the bowl as needed.

In a separate bowl, whisk the flour, baking soda, and salt together until they are combined. Add the dry ingredients into the wet ingredients and mix until they are just combined. Add the chocolate chips and pecans, then fold until everything is evenly distributed. The cookie dough will be quite thick.

Using a rubber spatula, spread the cookie dough evenly into the prepared skillet. Bake the cookie for 18 to 20 minutes, or until it's puffed, browned on the sides, and lightly browned on top. If you want your skillet cookie a little more cooked through, bake it for 22 to 25 minutes. Sprinkle the cookie with the flaky salt, if using.

Allow the cookie to slightly cool in the pan, set on a wire rack, before digging in. You can scoop or slice the cookie and serve it, or serve it with spoons and dig in together. Serve this cookie with the ice cream and chocolate syrup, if using; I always do. Cover leftovers, and store them in the refrigerator for up to 2 days.

VARIATION TIP: *Feel free to switch up the mix-ins and make this recipe your own! Try using M&M's® instead of chocolate chips, walnuts instead of pecans, or anything that you love to make this cookie exactly what you want! Just keep the total amount of mix-ins to around ½ cup or less.*

COOKING TIP: *For the prettiest, most photogenic skillet cookie, reserve a few chocolate chips and chopped pecans and gently press them into the top of the cookie dough just before baking it. You're guaranteed to have plenty of mix-ins showing in your finished product.*

¼ cup (57 g) unsalted butter, softened

¼ cup (55 g) dark brown sugar

¼ cup (50 g) granulated sugar

¼ cup (64 g) creamy peanut butter

1 tsp vanilla extract

2 tbsp (30 g) applesauce

¼ tsp baking soda

⅛ tsp fine sea salt

⅔ cup (83 g) all-purpose flour

3 oz (84 g) 70% cacao dark chocolate, chopped

Flaky sea salt, optional

PEANUT BUTTER CHOCOLATE CHUNK COOKIES

The only flavor that comes close to chocolate in my affections is peanut butter, so it's no surprise that a cookie recipe containing both of these things is high on my list of must-have recipes. When developing this recipe, I really wanted a peanut butter cookie base that would be just as delicious plain as it would be loaded with chocolate. In my opinion, a good peanut butter cookie should be soft and rich, but not so soft that it falls apart in your hands, and not so rich that you may as well just eat a spoonful of peanut butter. It also needs to be sweet, but not too sweet, and neither crunchy nor chewy, but somehow a little bit of both. Good peanut butter cookies are a rarity; these, however, are good peanut butter cookies.

Line a baking sheet with parchment paper, and set it aside.

In the bowl of a stand mixer fitted with the paddle attachment, or in a medium bowl using a handheld mixer, beat together the butter, dark brown sugar, and granulated sugar until the ingredients are combined and the mixture is fluffy and lighter in color, about 2 minutes. Add the peanut butter, vanilla, and applesauce, and mix until they are well combined, 1 to 2 minutes.

In a medium bowl, whisk together the baking soda, salt, and flour. Add the dry ingredients to the wet ingredients and mix until they are just combined; be sure not to overmix! Fold in the dark chocolate chunks until they are evenly dispersed.

Using a large (3-tablespoon [42-g]) spring-loaded cookie scoop, scoop the dough, roll it into balls, then place them on the prepared baking sheet. Loosely cover the dough with plastic wrap, and place it in the refrigerator to chill for at least 15 minutes or up to 24 hours.

Preheat the oven to 350°F (180°C) while the cookies chill. Bake the cookies for 9 to 10 minutes, or until they are lightly browned on the sides; the centers will look very soft. Remove the cookies from the oven, and sprinkle them with the flaky salt, if using. Allow the cookies to cool on the baking sheet for 5 minutes before transferring them to a wire rack to cool completely. Store leftovers in an airtight container for up to 3 days.

COOKING TIP: *If you like a crispier peanut butter cookie, bake yours for 11 to 13 minutes, until the edges of the cookies begin to darken.*

TOTAL TIME: 1 hour

MAKES: 8 cookies

FOR THE COOKIES

1¼ cups (150 g) all-purpose flour

½ tsp baking soda

1 tsp cream of tartar

¼ tsp ground cinnamon

¼ tsp fine sea salt

½ cup (113 g) unsalted butter, cubed

½ cup (110 g) dark brown sugar

¼ cup (50 g) granulated sugar

1 large egg yolk

1 tbsp (15 ml) bourbon

½ tbsp (8 g) sour cream, room temperature

FOR THE ROLLING MIXTURE

2 tbsp (24 g) granulated sugar

½ tsp ground cinnamon

BROWN BUTTER BOURBON SNICKERDOODLES

Traditional snickerdoodles taste like the best version of a cinnamon sugar cookie and are generally soft and chewy, thanks to the addition of cream of tartar. These snickerdoodles, however, take it a few steps further with the addition of both brown butter AND bourbon, which add richness and make for a warm and comforting combination that makes these cookies infinitely better than their standard counterpart. Trust me when I say that these are the sort of cookies that you want to make when you have people around to help you eat them, because they are DANGEROUS.

For the cookies, in a small bowl, whisk together the flour, baking soda, cream of tartar, cinnamon, and salt until they are well combined. Set aside the mixture.

Place the butter in a light-colored skillet. (A light-colored skillet will help you determine when the butter begins browning.) Melt the butter over medium heat, stirring constantly. Once melted, the butter will start to foam. Keep stirring. After 5 to 8 minutes, the butter will begin browning; you'll notice that lightly browned specks will begin to form at the bottom of the pan, and you'll start to smell a nutty aroma. Once the butter is browned, immediately remove it from the heat and pour it into a medium heat-safe bowl.

Add the dark brown sugar and granulated sugar to the brown butter, and whisk until they are combined. Add in the egg yolk, bourbon, and sour cream, and whisk until fully incorporated. Add in the dry ingredients and mix them with a silicone spatula until the flour is completely incorporated. Put the bowl in the fridge, and chill the dough for 15 minutes.

While the dough is chilling, preheat the oven to 350°F (180°C) and make the rolling mixture. Combine the sugar and cinnamon in a small bowl. Line a baking sheet with parchment paper, then set it aside.

Using a large (3-tablespoon [42-g]) spring-loaded cookie scoop, scoop the dough into eight pieces and roll them into balls. Toss the balls in the rolling mixture, then place them on the prepared baking sheet. Bake the cookies for 8 to 10 minutes, or until they are lightly browned on the sides; the centers will look very soft. Remove the pan from the oven, and cool the cookies on the baking sheet for 10 minutes before transferring them to a wire rack to cool completely.

Store leftover cookies in an airtight container at room temperature for up to 3 days.

VARIATION TIP: *For a more traditional (kid-friendly) version of these snickerdoodles, just replace the bourbon with vanilla extract!*

FOR THE COOKIES

½ cup + 2 tbsp (75 g) all-purpose flour

⅛ tsp baking soda

⅛ tsp fine sea salt

¼ tsp ground cinnamon

⅛ tsp ground ginger

⅛ tsp ground cardamom

⅛ tsp ground allspice

Pinch of black pepper

¼ cup (57 g) unsalted butter, softened

3 tbsp (36 g) granulated sugar, plus more for rolling

3 tbsp (21 g) powdered sugar

1 tbsp (15 g) applesauce

½ tsp vanilla bean paste

FOR THE VANILLA BEAN GLAZE, OPTIONAL

½ cup (60 g) powdered sugar

1–2 tbsp (15–30 ml) milk

½ tsp vanilla bean paste

VANILLA CHAI SUGAR COOKIES

These cookies came about one day when I was randomly experimenting in the kitchen. Since I know that chai spices are a great substitute for cinnamon, I was inspired by traditional snickerdoodle cookies to see what might happen if I flavored a chewy sugar cookie dough with chai spices. Spoiler: The result was amazing. These cookies are full of cozy, warm chai spices, are soft and chewy, and require very minimal chill time. And, as if that's not enough, you can top them off generously with a simple Vanilla Bean Glaze. YUM! Pair them with a piping hot cup of tea and thank me later.

For the cookies, line a baking sheet with parchment paper; set it aside.

In a medium bowl, whisk the flour, baking soda, salt, cinnamon, ginger, cardamom, allspice, and pepper together, then set aside the bowl.

In a separate medium bowl using a hand mixer, cream together the butter, granulated sugar, and powdered sugar on medium speed until smooth, 1 to 2 minutes. Add the applesauce and vanilla bean paste, and beat on medium until the ingredients are combined, about 30 seconds. Scrape down the sides and bottom of the bowl as needed. Pour the dry ingredients into the wet ingredients, then mix on low until they are just combined.

Place some granulated sugar in a small bowl. Using a small (1½-tablespoon [21-g]) spring-loaded cookie scoop, scoop the dough into six to eight pieces, roll them into balls, and toss them in the bowl of sugar. Place the balls on the prepared baking sheet. Place the baking sheet in the refrigerator uncovered for 15 minutes, to chill the dough. While the cookie dough chills, preheat the oven to 350°F (180°C).

Bake the cookies for 10 to 12 minutes, or until they are lightly browned on the sides; the centers will look very soft. Remove the cookies from the oven, and allow them to cool on the baking sheet for 10 minutes before transferring them to a wire rack to cool completely.

To make the glaze, if using, whisk the powdered sugar, 1 tablespoon (15 ml) of milk, and vanilla bean paste together. Add another tablespoon of milk to thin it out, if necessary. Drizzle the glaze on the cooled cookies. Store leftover cookies in an airtight container at room temperature for up to 3 days.

TOTAL TIME:
1 hour 30 minutes

MAKES: 8 cookies

FOR THE COOKIES

1 cup (120 g) all-purpose flour

¾ tsp baking powder

¼ tsp fine sea salt

⅓ cup (76 g) unsalted butter, softened

½ cup + 2 tbsp (125 g) granulated sugar

1 large egg, room temperature

½ tsp vanilla bean paste

¼ cup (60 ml) buttermilk, room temperature

FOR THE BLACK-AND-WHITE ICINGS

¾ cup (90 g) powdered sugar

½ tbsp + ¾ tsp (8 ml) light corn syrup

⅛ tsp vanilla bean paste

2 tbsp (30 ml) milk, divided

2 tbsp (10 g) unsweetened natural or Dutch-process cocoa powder

SMALL–BATCH BLACK–AND–WHITE COOKIES

These soft and tender black-and-white cookies are a bakery classic, especially in New York City. They're halfway between a cake and a cookie, loaded with vanilla flavor, and topped with sweet vanilla and chocolate icings. There's actually not a lot of work that goes into these cookies; just make sure you're patient and let the icing set to a nice matte finish before serving or storing the cookies. I promise they're worth the wait!

For the cookies, preheat the oven to 325°F (165°C). Line two baking sheets with parchment paper, then set them aside.

In a medium bowl, combine the flour, baking powder, and salt, then set aside the bowl. In the bowl of a stand mixer fitted with the paddle attachment, or in a large bowl using a handheld mixer, cream the butter and sugar together on medium speed until the mixture is light and fluffy, 2 to 3 minutes. Beat in the egg and vanilla bean paste until combined. With the mixer running on low speed, slowly stream in the buttermilk, and beat until it's completely incorporated. Add the dry ingredients and beat until they are just incorporated. The dough will be thinner than traditional cookie dough; it will be more like a thick, fluffy cake batter.

Using a large (3-tablespoon [42-g]) spring-loaded cookie scoop, portion out the dough into eight rounded dough balls, placing 4 on each prepared baking sheet. Bake the cookies for 12 to 14 minutes, or until the bottoms are a light golden brown. Cool the cookies on the pans for 10 minutes, then transfer them to a wire rack to cool completely.

To make the icing, in a medium bowl whisk together the powdered sugar, corn syrup, and vanilla bean paste until smooth. Thin it out with 2 to 3 teaspoons (10 to 15 ml) of milk, as needed. Place half of the icing in a separate bowl, then stir the cocoa powder into one bowl. Thin the chocolate icing with 2 to 3 teaspoons (10 to 15 ml) of milk, as needed, until it's the same consistency as the white icing.

To frost the cookies, flip each cookie over so that the flat side is facing up. Frost one-half of each cookie with the white icing. After the icing has dried, frost the other half with the chocolate icing. Allow the cookies to rest at room temperature until the icing is completely dry to the touch. Store leftovers in an airtight container at room temperature for up to 5 days.

½ cup (60 g) all-purpose flour

¼ cup (57 g) unsalted butter, softened

¼ cup (55 g) light brown sugar

2 tbsp (25 g) granulated sugar

½ tsp vanilla extract

¼ tsp fine sea salt

¼ cup (44 g) semisweet chocolate chips

4 oz (115 g) 55% cacao semisweet chocolate, finely chopped

½ tbsp (7 ml) canola oil

1 oz (28 g) 70% cacao dark chocolate, melted, optional

CHOCOLATE CHIP COOKIE DOUGH TRUFFLES

I love chocolate chip cookie dough; it's honestly the best thing ever. And, I have no shame in admitting that I eat it by the spoonful whenever I'm making cookies. I think it's almost better than the baked version. That's why I adapted my favorite cookie dough recipe for these cookie dough truffles. This edible cookie dough is an eggless version that is totally safe to eat; it also uses heat-treated flour to kill off any bacteria. The result is little delicious nuggets of edible chocolate chip cookie dough covered with a chocolate coating. What's not to love!?

Preheat the oven to 350°F (180°C). Line a rimmed baking sheet with parchment paper and evenly spread the flour onto the sheet. Bake it in the preheated oven for 5 to 7 minutes, then set it aside to cool. Heat-treating the flour this way kills any potential bacteria!

Line another baking sheet with parchment paper, and set it aside.

In a medium bowl using a handheld mixer, beat the butter, brown sugar, and granulated sugar together on medium speed until the mixture is light and fluffy, about 2 minutes. Add the vanilla and salt, and beat until they are incorporated. Add in the flour and chocolate chips, and mix on low speed until they are just combined.

Using a small (1½-tablespoon [21-g]) spring-loaded cookie scoop, portion out the dough into eight pieces and roll them into balls. Place the balls on the prepared baking sheet. Loosely cover the dough with plastic wrap, and place the sheet in the refrigerator for 30 minutes, to chill the dough.

In a small saucepan, bring 2 inches (5 cm) of water to a simmer over medium heat. Add the semisweet chocolate and canola oil to a medium heat-safe bowl, then set the bowl over the simmering water. Do not let the bottom of the bowl touch the water. Stir until the chocolate is completely melted, then remove it from the heat, and set it aside to cool slightly.

Remove the cookie dough truffles from the fridge and dip them into the melted chocolate using a fork or chocolate-dipping tool. Place them on the prepared baking sheet, and drizzle them with the melted dark chocolate, if using. Refrigerate the truffles for at least 15 minutes to allow the chocolate coating to set before eating them.

These cookie dough truffles will remain fresh in an airtight container in the refrigerator for up to 1 week.

TOTAL TIME: 2 hours

MAKES: 6–8 cookies

1 cup (125 g) all-purpose flour

¼ tsp baking soda

⅛ tsp fine sea salt

1 tbsp (5 g) blood orange zest

½ cup (100 g) granulated sugar, plus more for rolling

¼ cup (57 g) unsalted butter, softened

1 tbsp (15 ml) freshly squeezed blood orange juice

1 large egg, room temperature

½ tsp vanilla bean paste

½ tsp orange extract

Red and/or orange gel food coloring, optional, see Ingredient Tip

Powdered sugar, for rolling

INGREDIENT TIP: *Blood oranges can vary in their color intensity, from almost as pale as regular oranges to that deep maroon color they're most famous for. Because of this, you might want to add a drop or two of red and/or orange food coloring into the dough if you find your blood orange juice isn't adding enough color on its own.*

BLOOD ORANGE CRINKLE COOKIES

Blood oranges are truly one of the most visually alluring fruits around. The flesh is a deep maroon—a color seemingly like no other—and the rind is orange with patches of faded pinkish-red. And, when you rub a bit of their zest into the sugar of your crinkle cookie dough and squeeze a bit of their juice in for good measure, the result is one of the most exciting-looking (and tasting) crinkle cookies you'll come across. The deep, reddish-orange crevices are surrounded by bright white, cloudlike patches of powdered sugar and have crispy edges, soft, chewy centers, and the brightest orange flavor. Sign me up, please!

Whisk the flour, baking soda, and salt together in a medium bowl, then set it aside.

In a separate medium bowl, combine the zest and granulated sugar. Using your fingers, rub the zest into the sugar until the mixture is well combined and fragrant. Add the butter. Using a handheld mixer, beat the butter and sugar together until the mixture is combined and fluffy, about 2 minutes. Add the orange juice, egg, vanilla bean paste, orange extract, and food coloring, if using, and beat until combined. Don't worry if the mixture looks a little curdled!

With the mixer running on low speed, slowly add the dry ingredients to the wet ingredients until the ingredients are combined. Cover the dough tightly with plastic wrap, and chill it in the refrigerator for at least 1 hour or up to 24 hours.

Remove the cookie dough from the refrigerator; let it sit at room temperature for 10 minutes. Preheat the oven to 350°F (180°C). Line two baking sheets with parchment paper, then set them aside. Place some granulated sugar in a small bowl and the powdered sugar in another bowl.

Using a large (3-tablespoon [42-g]) spring-loaded cookie scoop, scoop out six to eight portions of the cookie dough and roll them into balls. Roll each ball very lightly in the granulated sugar, then generously in the powdered sugar. Place the cookies 2 inches (5 cm) apart on the prepared baking sheets.

Bake the cookies for 10 to 12 minutes. If the cookies aren't really spreading by minute 9, remove them from the oven and lightly bang the baking sheet on the counter two to three times; this will help initiate that spread. Return the cookies to the oven for a couple more minutes. The cookies will be thick regardless, though they'll deflate a little as they cool.

Cool the cookies for 5 minutes on the baking sheet, then transfer them to a wire rack to cool completely. Store leftovers in an airtight container at room temperature for up to 4 days.

TOTAL TIME: 45 minutes

MAKES: 4–6 cookies

1½ oz (42 g) 70% cacao dark chocolate, chopped

1 tbsp (14 g) unsalted butter

3 tbsp (36 g) granulated sugar

1 tbsp (15 ml) water

½ tsp canola oil

½ tbsp (7 ml) milk

½ tsp vanilla extract

5 tbsp (38 g) all-purpose flour

1 tbsp (5 g) unsweetened natural or Dutch-process cocoa powder

1 tsp baking powder

⅛ tsp fine sea salt

1 tsp espresso powder

2 tbsp (22 g) chocolate chips, for topping

Flaky sea salt, optional

DOUBLE CHOCOLATE ESPRESSO COOKIES

Two warnings about these cookies: Don't give them to young children before bedtime, and don't leave them lying around (if you want any left for yourself). These cookies are crisp on the edges and chewy in the middle, with pockets of melted chocolate chips on top. They're basically a brownie cookie, and the added espresso powder makes the chocolate magically more chocolaty, with a slight mocha taste and no extra sweetness, making them grown-up cookies. They're decadent and rich, and best when accompanied with a glass of milk.

Preheat the oven to 350°F (180°C). Line a baking sheet with parchment paper, then set it aside.

Place the dark chocolate and butter in a heat-safe bowl and set it over a pan of gently simmering water to create a double boiler; stir until the mixture is completely smooth and melted. Alternatively, melt the chocolate and butter in the microwave, heating it in 30-second intervals and mixing thoroughly between each interval. Once the chocolate is fully melted, remove the bowl from the heat, and stir in the sugar.

Add the water, oil, milk, and vanilla, and whisk until well combined. Then, add the flour, cocoa powder, baking powder, salt, and espresso powder, and stir until combined. The batter will look a little thin when compared to traditional cookie dough (it will be similar to a thick brownie batter). Using a small (1½-tablespoon [21-g]) spring-loaded cookie scoop, scoop the dough onto the prepared baking sheet. Press a few chocolate chips into the tops of each cookie, then bake them for 7 to 9 minutes, or until the edges of the cookies look slightly set.

Remove the cookies from the oven and sprinkle the flaky sea salt on top, if using. Allow the cookies to cool on the baking sheet for 10 minutes before transferring them to a wire rack to cool completely. Store leftover cookies in an airtight container at room temperature for up to 3 days.

VARIATION TIP: *You can make these cookies triple or even quadruple chocolate espresso cookies by mixing your chocolates. Try half white chocolate chips, half semisweet, or even a mixture of white, semisweet, and dark chocolate!*

TOTAL TIME: 45 minutes

MAKES: 2 cookies

3 tbsp (42 g) unsalted butter, softened

¼ cup + 1 tbsp (60 g) granulated sugar

2 tsp (10 g) light brown sugar

1 tbsp (15 g) applesauce

1 tsp water

½ tsp vanilla extract

½ cup (60 g) all-purpose flour

⅛ tsp fine sea salt

⅛ tsp baking soda

1½ oz (42 g) 70% cacao dark chocolate, chopped

Flaky sea salt, optional

PAN-BANGING CHOCOLATE CHUNK COOKIES FOR TWO

If you follow me on social media, then chances are you've seen or heard me rave about my friend Sarah Kieffer's pan-banging cookies. Thanks to a somewhat unusual technique, these thin cookies have buttery, crispy edges with picture-perfect ridges and a soft, gooey center. The trick that gives them their unique texture? Banging the sheet pan every few minutes as the cookies bake—so that the cookies deflate and give way to their distinctive crinkled texture. The recipe you see before you is basically a scaled-down version of Sarah's already perfect recipe; it yields just two large cookies, perfect for a little celebratory indulgence without going completely overboard. (I'll let you decide whether or not you want to share!) So, find something to celebrate today: a major milestone, something crossed off your to-do list, or simply the fact that it's a Friday.

Preheat the oven to 350°F (180°C). Line a baking sheet with aluminum foil, dull-side up, and set it aside.

In a medium bowl using a handheld mixer, beat the butter, granulated sugar, and brown sugar on medium speed until light and fluffy, about 2 minutes. Add the applesauce, water, and vanilla, and mix on low to combine. Add the flour, salt, and baking soda and, again, mix on low until the ingredients are combined. Add the chocolate and fold it into the batter, using a silicone spatula.

Form the dough into two 4-ounce (115-g) balls. Place them an equal distance apart on the prepared pan and transfer them to the freezer for 15 minutes.

Place the chilled baking sheet in the oven, and bake the cookies for 10 minutes, until they are puffed slightly in the center. Lift the side of the baking sheet up about 4 inches (10 cm) and gently let it drop down against the oven rack, so the edges of the cookies set and the inside falls back down (this will feel wrong, but trust me). After the cookies puff up again in 2 minutes, repeat lifting and dropping the pan. Repeat a few more times to create ridges around the edge of the cookie. Bake the cookies for 16 to 18 minutes total, until the cookies have spread out and the edges are golden brown but the centers are much lighter and not fully cooked.

Transfer the baking sheet to a wire rack, and sprinkle the cookies with the flaky salt, if using. Let the cookies cool completely before removing them from the pan.

BROWNIES, BARS & SQUARES, OH MY!

Let me just start by saying that I take brownie and bar desserts very seriously. I mean . . . hello, I devoted my first cookbook, *Even Better Brownies*, to them! There's just something about the simplicity of mixing up a few ingredients and pouring or pressing them into a pan that can't be beat. And, while brownies and bars are great for family get-togethers, potlucks, or pretty much any other time you need enough dessert to feed a crowd . . . they're not exactly the best dessert to make when that random sweet tooth craving hits because of all the leftovers. Fortunately, that's not something you need to worry about with any of the recipes in this chapter.

One of the things I love the most about this chapter, besides the fact that it contains some of the easiest recipes in this entire book, is that every single recipe can be made in one pan: a 9 x 5–inch (23 x 13–cm) loaf pan. Not only is it the most common loaf pan size, but it also yields the perfect number of treats; talk about a serious win-win!

The brownies, bars, and squares in this chapter are sure to become your go-to small-batch dessert recipes, not only because of their ease, but also because of how quickly they come together and how mouthwateringly delicious they all are. There are the Fluffernutter Blondies (page 70), which combine my love of peanut butter and marshmallow creme into one ooey-gooey treat. The Raspberry Crumb Bars (page 78) have an insanely addictive base and crumb topping and can be customized with your favorite fruit. And, don't even get me started on the Small-Batch Fruity Pebbles™ Treats (page 85), which get made so regularly in my apartment that I could probably make them with my eyes closed.

TIPS & TECHNIQUES

Brownies and bars are easier and more forgiving than many other baked goods. Still, these tips and techniques will ensure you get the best results possible.

PREPARING LOAF PANS: A sheet of parchment paper will ensure that brownies and bars come out of their pans whole and perfect. To line the pans, grease the empty pan and press the parchment paper over the greased surface, making sure it lies flat so no batter can flow underneath. Some recipes will also direct you to grease the parchment paper.

THE RIGHT LOAF PAN: Make sure you're using an aluminum or metal baking pan. Aluminum is an excellent heat conductor, which means baked goods will bake and brown evenly. Glass bakeware, in comparison, is heavier than aluminum and is an insulator, rather than a conductor. This means that glass is slow to heat and, once it's hot, it retains that heat for longer. This can result in uneven baking, because by the time the interior is baked through, the exterior is often overcooked, dry, or dark.

TESTING FOR DONENESS: Brownies and bars are sensitive creatures: a few minutes too long in the oven, and you'll wave goodbye to their ideal texture. For the best results, check for doneness five minutes before the recommended bake time in the recipe since every oven—and baking pan—is different.

STORAGE: Unless otherwise noted, these recipes can be stored at room temperature in an airtight container and will generally stay fresh for up to 3 or 4 days.

TOTAL TIME: 1 hour

MAKES: 8 brownies

2 oz (56 g) 70% cacao dark chocolate, chopped

1 tsp espresso powder

3 tbsp (15 g) unsweetened natural or Dutch-process cocoa powder

½ cup (113 g) unsalted butter

6 tbsp (75 g) granulated sugar

¼ cup (55 g) dark brown sugar

1 tsp vanilla extract

½ tsp fine sea salt

2 large eggs

⅓ cup (45 g) all-purpose flour

Flaky sea salt, optional

SMALL-BATCH FUDGE BROWNIES

As universally loved as brownies are, they are not without controversy. Fudgy or cakey? Crispy edge or gooey middle piece? Cocoa brownies or chopped chocolate? Butter or oil? It can be a wild brownie recipe world out there. But no need to stress, because I've got the only brownie recipe you need. This fudge brownie recipe is actually a scaled-down version of one of the most popular recipes on my blog and in my first cookbook! They are made with both real chocolate AND cocoa powder, which yields brownies that are dense, chocolaty, and extremely fudgy. It's time to say goodbye to mediocre brownies and HELLO to the most amazing fudge brownies ever.

Preheat the oven to 350°F (180°C). Lightly grease a 9 x 5–inch (23 x 13–cm) loaf pan with butter or cooking spray, then line it with parchment paper, leaving an overhang on the two long sides. Lightly grease the parchment with butter or nonstick cooking spray, then set aside the pan.

In a small heat-safe bowl, combine the chocolate, espresso powder, and cocoa powder, and set aside the bowl.

Add the butter to a small saucepan over medium heat, and cook the butter until it just comes to a vigorous simmer, about 3 minutes, stirring often. Immediately pour the hot butter over the chocolate mixture, and let it sit for 1 minute. Whisk until the chocolate is completely smooth and melted, then set it aside.

Using an electric hand mixer, whisk together the granulated sugar, brown sugar, vanilla, salt, and eggs for *precisely* 5 minutes on high; I set a timer. With the mixer on, pour in the slightly cooled chocolate mixture; mix until the batter is smooth, about 2 minutes.

Add in the flour, and use a rubber spatula to gently fold it in until it is just combined. Pour the batter into the prepared baking pan, and smooth the top with a spatula. Bake the brownies for 20 minutes, then remove the pan from the oven and slam it on a flat surface two to three times (this deflates the brownies slightly, giving them a more even texture and encourages that beautiful crackly top). Return the pan to the oven, and bake the brownies until a toothpick inserted into the center of the brownies comes out fudgy, but the edges look cooked through, about 5 minutes. The center of the brownies will seem underbaked, but the brownies will continue to cook and set as they cool.

Sprinkle the top of the brownies with the flaky salt, if using, and allow the brownies to cool completely in the pan.

Use the parchment paper to lift the cooled brownies out of the pan; cut them into eight bars. Cover leftover brownies, and store them in an airtight container at room temperature for 2 to 3 days.

TOTAL TIME: 1 hour

MAKES: 8 blondies

6 tbsp (85 g) unsalted butter, melted

¼ cup (55 g) light brown sugar

¼ cup (55 g) dark brown sugar

3 tbsp (36 g) granulated sugar

1 large egg, room temperature

1 tsp vanilla extract

¾ cup + 2 tbsp (110 g) all-purpose flour

¾ tsp cornstarch

¼ tsp baking powder

½ tsp fine sea salt

2 tbsp (32 g) creamy peanut butter

2 tbsp (20 g) marshmallow fluff

FLUFFERNUTTER BLONDIES

Calling blondies chocolate-free brownies fails to recognize what makes them so uniquely crave-worthy; their flavor oomph comes from brown sugar. Normal blondies are delicious in their own right, but these Fluffernutter Blondies . . . they're next level. Now, if you're sitting there thinking, "What the heck is a fluffernutter?" then let me enlighten you. A fluffernutter is a sandwich made with peanut butter and marshmallow creme, usually served on white bread. Some people even grill it like you would a grilled cheese sandwich. It's basically a dessert sandwich, if you will. I took all the flavors of that gooey sandwich and developed an ooey-gooey peanut butter marshmallow blondie that both kids and adults will love!

Preheat the oven to 350°F (180°C). Lightly grease a 9 x 5–inch (23 x 13–cm) loaf pan with butter or cooking spray, then line it with parchment paper, leaving an overhang on the two long sides. Lightly grease the parchment with butter or nonstick cooking spray, then set aside the pan.

In a medium bowl, whisk together the butter, light brown sugar, dark brown sugar, and granulated sugar until combined. Add the egg and vanilla, and beat until the mixture is lighter in color, about 2 minutes. Add the flour, cornstarch, baking powder, and salt, and mix until just combined.

Transfer the batter to the prepared pan and top it with dollops of the peanut butter and marshmallow fluff. Drag a skewer or toothpick through the dollops to make a marbled effect in the batter. Bake the blondies for 25 to 30 minutes, until the top and edges are set and golden. Remove the pan from the oven, and allow the blondies to cool in the pan completely before removing and slicing them.

Cover leftover blondies, and store them in an airtight container at room temperature for 3 to 4 days.

TOTAL TIME: 45 minutes

MAKES: 8 cookie bars

¾ cup (90 g) all-purpose flour

¼ tsp baking powder

¼ tsp baking soda

¼ tsp fine sea salt

¼ cup (57 g) unsalted butter, softened

¼ cup (55 g) dark brown sugar

3 tbsp (36 g) granulated sugar

1 large egg yolk

½ tsp vanilla extract

4 oz (115 g) 70% cacao dark chocolate, chopped

⅓ cup (40 g) toasted walnuts, chopped

Flaky sea salt, optional

CHOCOLATE CHUNK WALNUT COOKIE BARS

What do you do when the craving for chocolate chunk cookies strikes, but you just don't have the time or energy to scoop, roll, and bake multiple batches of your favorite treat? Cue these Chocolate Chunk Walnut Cookie Bars! These are the best small-batch cookie bars EVER. The recipe is easy to make (10 minutes to mix, 20 minutes to bake), and it results in a gooey, chewy, doughy yet fully-cooked chocolate chunk cookie bar—studded with toasted walnuts—that is 100 percent irresistible. Walnuts not your thing? Feel free to replace them with your favorite nut or just leave them out altogether!

Preheat the oven to 350°F (180°C). Grease a 9 x 5–inch (23 x 13–cm) loaf pan with butter or nonstick cooking spray, then line the pan with parchment paper, leaving an overhang on the two long sides. Grease the parchment paper with butter or nonstick cooking spray, then set aside the pan.

In a small bowl, whisk together the flour, baking powder, baking soda, and salt. Set aside the bowl.

In a medium bowl using an electric hand mixer, cream together the butter, dark brown sugar, and granulated sugar until the ingredients are combined and fluffy, about 3 minutes. Add the egg yolk and vanilla, and mix until they're incorporated. Add the dry ingredients and mix until they are just combined. Fold the chocolate and walnuts into the dough.

Gently press the dough into the prepared pan in an even layer. Bake the bars for 15 to 18 minutes, or until the top is light golden brown and slightly firm to the touch. Do not overbake; I even recommend slightly underbaking these! If using, sprinkle the flaky salt on top right after the pan comes out of the oven. Allow the cookie bars to cool completely in the pan before removing and slicing them.

Cover leftover bars, and store them in an airtight container at room temperature for 2 to 3 days.

TOTAL TIME:
3 hours 30 minutes

MAKES: 8 bars

FOR THE GRAHAM CRACKER CRUST

1½ cups (150 g) graham cracker crumbs, approximately 9 full-sized sheets

¼ cup (55 g) light brown sugar

⅛ tsp fine sea salt

5 tbsp (75 g) unsalted butter, melted

FOR THE VANILLA BEAN CHEESECAKE FILLING

1 tsp powdered gelatin

¾ cup + 2 tbsp (210 ml) heavy cream, divided

8 oz (226 g) cream cheese, softened, see Ingredient Tip

¼ cup + 2 tbsp (75 g) granulated sugar

1 tsp vanilla bean paste

¼ tsp fine sea salt

INGREDIENT TIP: *It's extremely important that the cream cheese be room temperature and properly softened before you start, so that there are no chunks in the finished cheesecake. If you cannot beat the cream cheese to a smooth consistency, let it sit at room temperature for 15 minutes, then beat it again.*

NO-BAKE VANILLA BEAN CHEESECAKE BARS

A slice of luxuriously rich cheesecake has become one of my favorite guilty pleasures. Despite this love of cheesecake, I rarely make it at home, because it can be a bit fussy. These No-Bake Vanilla Bean Cheesecake Bars, however, are a completely different story. You get all the great flavor of cheesecake without the fuss of making a big cheesecake. Talk about a total game-changer!

Lightly grease a 9 x 5–inch (23 x 13–cm) loaf pan with butter or cooking spray, then line it with parchment paper, leaving an overhang on the two long sides. Lightly grease the parchment with butter or nonstick cooking spray, then set aside the pan.

To make the crust, whisk together the graham cracker crumbs, brown sugar, and salt in a medium bowl. Add the butter and mix to combine; the mixture should have the consistency of wet sand. Pour the crust into the prepared pan and pat it down until smooth using the bottom of a flat glass or a measuring cup, ensuring that it has an even thickness. Place the crust in the freezer while you prepare the filling.

To make the cheesecake filling, in a small saucepan over low heat, dissolve the gelatin in ¼ cup (60 ml) of the heavy cream. Set it aside.

In the bowl of a stand mixer fitted with the whisk attachment, or using an electric hand mixer, whip the remaining ½ cup + 2 tablespoons (150 ml) of heavy cream until medium peaks form. The cream will start to thicken, become smooth, and leave trails in the mixture. To test, the cream is whipped when you lift up your whisk and peaks form, but the peaks curl down slightly at the ends. Transfer the cream into a bowl and set it aside.

In the same bowl used to whip the cream (there's no need to wash it), whip the cream cheese and granulated sugar until smooth, about 3 minutes. Add the vanilla bean paste and salt, and beat to incorporate the ingredients, then add the gelatin and cream mixture and mix well.

Remove the bowl from the mixer and, using a spatula, gently fold the whipped cream into the cream cheese mixture. Spoon the filling over the prepared base, tapping the pan to remove any bubbles, then smooth the top with an offset spatula.

Refrigerate the cheesecake for at least 3 hours, or until it's firm. Using the parchment paper as a sling, remove the cheesecake from the pan. Run a knife through hot water, dry it, then cut the cheesecake into 8 squares.

Cover leftover bars, and store them in an airtight container in the refrigerator for 5 to 7 days.

3 tbsp (23 g) all-purpose flour

3 tbsp (15 g) unsweetened natural or Dutch-process cocoa powder, see Ingredient Tip

⅛ tsp espresso powder

⅛ tsp baking powder

¼ tsp fine sea salt

6 tbsp (85 g) unsalted butter, cubed

3½ oz (99 g) 70% cacao dark chocolate, finely chopped

1 tsp canola oil

¾ cup (150 g) granulated sugar

1 large egg

1 large egg yolk

1 tbsp (15 ml) vanilla extract

½ cup (57 g) coarsely chopped pecans, divided

Flaky sea salt, optional

INGREDIENT TIP: *I love using Dutch-process cocoa powder because it has a more intense dark chocolate flavor than natural cocoa powder. But, if you like your brownies more on the milk chocolate side, then semi-sweet chocolate and natural cocoa will work just fine.*

BROWN BUTTER PECAN BROWNIES

These brownies have it all. They're rich, a little fudgy, and have a crisp, almost meringue-like top. If you follow me on social media, you know that browning butter is kind of my secret trick to improving the flavor of just about every classic baked good, and these brownies are no exception. Browning adds a subtle nuttiness that complements the pecans and a depth of flavor you just don't get with regular butter. It also brings out some of the darker notes in the chocolate, which leaves you with rich, fudgy homemade brownies that will leave everyone wondering what the secret ingredient is.

Preheat the oven to 350°F (180°C). Lightly grease a 9 x 5–inch (23 x 13–cm) loaf pan with butter or cooking spray then line it with parchment paper, leaving an overhang on the two long sides. Lightly grease the parchment with butter or nonstick cooking spray, then set it aside.

In a small bowl, whisk together the flour, cocoa powder, espresso powder, baking powder, and salt. Set aside the bowl.

Place the butter in a light-colored skillet. (A light-colored skillet will help you determine when the butter begins browning.) Melt the butter over medium heat, stirring it constantly. Once melted, the butter will start to foam. Keep stirring. After 5 to 8 minutes, the butter will begin browning; you'll notice that lightly browned specks begin to form at the bottom of the pan, and you'll start to smell a nutty aroma. Once the butter is browned, immediately remove it from the heat, and pour it in a heat-safe bowl. Set it aside.

Place the chocolate and canola oil in a heat-safe bowl, and set it over a pan of gently simmering water to create a double boiler; stir until the mixture is completely smooth and melted. Alternatively, melt the chocolate and oil in the microwave, heating in 30-second intervals and mixing thoroughly between each interval. Once the chocolate is fully melted, remove the bowl from the heat, and stir in the browned butter and the granulated sugar. The mixture will be slightly grainy and paste-like.

Whisk in the egg, egg yolk, and vanilla until the batter is smooth and shiny. Add the dry ingredients, and stir until they are just incorporated. Stir in ¼ cup + 2 tablespoons (43 g) of the pecans until they are evenly dispersed. Spread the batter into the prepared pan, using an offset spatula to smooth the batter into the corners. Sprinkle the top with the remaining 2 tablespoons (14 g) of pecans.

Bake the brownies for 28 to 30 minutes, or until the top is shiny and crackly and a toothpick inserted near the center comes out mostly clean. Top with the flaky salt, if using. Allow the brownies to cool in the pan on a wire rack before slicing them into squares.

Cover leftover brownies, and store them in an airtight container at room temperature for 3 to 4 days.

RASPBERRY CRUMB BARS

TOTAL TIME: 1 hour

MAKES: 8 bars

FOR THE CRUST AND CRUMB TOPPING

1 cup + 2 tbsp (90 g) old-fashioned oats

1 cup + 2 tbsp (135 g) all-purpose flour

½ cup (110 g) light brown sugar

¼ cup (55 g) dark brown sugar

½ tsp baking powder

¼ tsp fine sea salt

9 tbsp (127 g) unsalted butter, melted

FOR THE RASPBERRY FILLING

9 oz (250 g) fresh raspberries, see Ingredient Tip

3 tbsp (36 g) granulated sugar

1 tbsp (8 g) all-purpose flour

½ tbsp (4 g) cornstarch

1 tbsp (15 ml) freshly squeezed lemon juice

I have strong opinions about fruit bars. I like them to be soft, not crunchy. Fruity, but not overloaded with fruit. And, overall, not too cloyingly sweet. These Raspberry Crumb Bars tick all of the boxes. They have a soft, brown sugar and oatmeal cookie-like base and a thick, sweet-tart but not overwhelming layer of raspberries in the middle. It's all tucked in by a layer of those streusel-like crumbs on top. These bars are simple, easy, and truly the BEST; a delicious breakfast or afternoon treat!

Preheat the oven to 350°F (180°C). Lightly grease a 9 x 5–inch (23 x 13–cm) loaf pan with butter or cooking spray, then line it with parchment paper, leaving an overhang on the two long sides. Lightly grease the parchment with butter or nonstick cooking spray, then set aside the pan.

For the crust and topping, in a large bowl, whisk together the oats, flour, light brown sugar, dark brown sugar, baking powder, and salt. Add the butter and stir together until the ingredients are combined into a crumble-like mixture. Press two-thirds of the crumble into the bottom of the prepared baking pan, and parbake the crust for 10 minutes; the crust will still look unbaked, but the edges should start to look puffy and raised.

While the crust is baking, make the filling. Mix the raspberries with the sugar, flour, cornstarch, and lemon juice; I like to mash some of the raspberries to help release some of their juices. Set aside the filling. Remove the crust from the oven, and arrange the raspberry filling in an even layer on top of the parbaked bottom layer. Sprinkle the filling with the remaining crumble mixture, and bake the bars for 25 to 30 minutes, or until the crumble is golden and the filling is bubbling.

Cool the bars in the pan on a wire rack for at least 1 hour before removing the bars and slicing them. I like to chill them for a few hours to help get them really solid. Cover leftover bars, and store them in an airtight container in the refrigerator for 2 to 3 days.

INGREDIENT TIP: *You can use frozen raspberries instead of fresh raspberries if that's all you have on hand. Simply place the raspberries in a colander. Run warm water over them for a minute, and then let the liquid drain out for about an hour, until the raspberries soften and are thoroughly drained. Then proceed with the recipe as written.*

TOTAL TIME: 3 hours

MAKES: 8 bars

FOR THE SHORTBREAD CRUST

6 tbsp (85 g) unsalted butter, melted

3 tbsp (36 g) granulated sugar

½ tsp vanilla extract

⅛ tsp fine sea salt

¾ cup + 1 tbsp (101 g) all-purpose flour

FOR THE LEMON FILLING

¾ cup (150 g) granulated sugar

2 tbsp (15 g) all-purpose flour

2 large eggs, room temperature

⅓ cup + 2 tsp (90 ml) freshly squeezed lemon juice, about 2 whole lemons, see Ingredient Tip

Powdered sugar, for dusting, optional

INGREDIENT TIP: *For these lemon bars to have a nice citrus flavor, you need to use fresh lemons; avoid the imitation lemon juice that comes in a bottle. When choosing lemons, make sure to look for ones that are fragrant and have bright yellow skins. They should be firm, plump, and heavy for their size. Avoid lemons that have blemishes, soft spots, or green spots, or any that are hard and wrinkled.*

SMALL-BATCH LEMON BARS

Lemon bars are one of the EASIEST desserts to make and they're guaranteed to bring a smile to your face. I love the soft lemon filling paired with the buttery, crisp shortbread crust. The flavor is beyond delicious: It's so bright and zingy, with all the lemon from the juice and zest. They're simply irresistible! I think my favorite part of these Small-Batch Lemon Bars is how easy they are to make. Instead of making a proper curd, these bars have a simple filling mix that gets poured over the base and bakes up like curd. The hardest part of this recipe is waiting for the bars to cool and finish setting, but I have faith in you!

Preheat the oven to 325°F (165°C). Lightly grease a 9 x 5–inch (23 x 13–cm) loaf pan with butter or cooking spray, then line it with parchment paper, leaving an overhang on the two long sides. Lightly grease the parchment with butter or nonstick cooking spray, then set aside the pan.

For the crust, in a medium bowl, mix together the butter, sugar, vanilla, and salt. Add the flour and stir until it's completely combined. The dough will be thick. Press the dough firmly into the prepared pan, making sure the layer of crust is nice and even. Bake the crust for 20 minutes, or until the edges are lightly browned. Remove the pan from the oven and, using a fork, gently poke holes all over the top of the warm crust, but not all the way through the crust. Set it aside.

For the filling, in a medium bowl, sift together the sugar and flour. Whisk in the eggs, then the lemon juice until the ingredients are completely combined. Pour the filling over the warm crust. Bake the bars for 20 to 22 minutes, or until the center is relatively set and no longer jiggles. Give the pan a light tap to test. Remove the bars from the oven and cool them completely at room temperature, about 2 hours. I like to then stick them in the refrigerator for 1 to 2 hours until they are chilled, to make slicing them easier, but this is optional.

Once the bars are cool, lift the parchment paper out of the pan using the overhang on the sides. Dust the top of the bars with the powdered sugar, if using, and cut them into squares before serving. For neat squares, wipe the knife clean between each cut. Leftover lemon bars can be stored in an airtight container in the refrigerator for up to 5 days.

MAKE-AHEAD INSTRUCTIONS: *Lemon bars can be frozen for up to 3 months. Cut the cooled bars (without the powdered sugar topping) into squares, then place them onto a baking sheet. Freeze the bars for 1 hour. Individually wrap each bar in aluminum foil or plastic wrap, then place them into a large bag or freezer container. Thaw the bars in the refrigerator, then dust them with the powdered sugar before serving.*

TOTAL TIME: 1 hour

MAKES: 8 brownies

⅓ cup (42 g) all-purpose flour

¼ cup (55 g) light brown sugar

½ cup (100 g) granulated sugar

3 tbsp (15 g) unsweetened natural or Dutch-process cocoa powder

¼ tsp fine sea salt

⅛ tsp baking powder

6 tbsp (85 g) unsalted butter, melted

1 large egg, room temperature

1 large egg yolk, room temperature

½ tsp vanilla extract

2 tbsp (32 g) cookie butter, see Ingredient Tip

COOKIE BUTTER SWIRL BROWNIES

These brownies are rich, sweet, chocolaty, and made all the more indulgent with a decadent swirl of cookie butter. If you've never had cookie butter, you need to go to the store ASAP and get a jar or two! It's basically a sweet spread—think Nutella—that's made with speculoos cookies. It's as amazing as it sounds! You'll be glad you made only an eight-serving batch, because these are impossible to stop eating (at least for me).

Preheat the oven to 350°F (180°C). Lightly grease a 9 x 5–inch (23 x 13–cm) loaf pan with butter or cooking spray, then line it with parchment paper, leaving an overhang on the two long sides. Lightly grease the parchment with butter or nonstick cooking spray, then set aside the pan.

In a large bowl, whisk together the flour, light brown sugar, granulated sugar, cocoa powder, salt, and baking powder. In a medium bowl, whisk the butter, egg, egg yolk, and vanilla until the ingredients are well combined. Add the wet ingredients to the dry ingredients, and mix them until they are just combined.

Transfer the brownie batter to the prepared pan. Top the batter with random dollops of the cookie butter. Using a knife, swirl the cookie butter into the batter. Bake the bars for 25 to 27 minutes, or until the brownies are just set and a toothpick inserted into the center comes out with a few moist crumbs.

Remove the brownies from the oven, and place the pan on a wire rack. Cool the brownies completely in the pan before cutting them into squares.

Cover leftover brownies, and store them at room temperature for up to 5 days.

INGREDIENT TIP: *Some brands of cookie butter are slightly thicker than others. You might find it easier to swirl the cookie butter into the brownie batter if you warm it up and melt it slightly!*

TOTAL TIME: 1 hour

MAKES: 8 bars

3 tbsp (42 g) unsalted butter

⅛ tsp fine sea salt

½ tsp vanilla extract

6½ oz (186 g) mini marshmallows, divided

3 cups (84 g) Fruity Pebbles cereal

1 cup + 1 tbsp (35 g) Rice Krispies cereal

COOKING TIP: *After you add the marshmallows, be sure to keep the heat on medium-low or lower. The residual heat of the pan should be enough to melt them. If your marshmallow is exposed to heat that's too high or exposed to heat for too long, you'll end up with treats hard enough to break your teeth!*

SMALL-BATCH FRUITY PEBBLES™ TREATS

We are all familiar with Rice Krispies® treats, no doubt. The chewy and crispy texture and super sweet flavor are so delightful, and, when prepared well, these simple goodies are as good as gourmet! As much as I love the classic treat, it's fun to switch things up now and then. That's why my Small-Batch Fruity Pebbles™ Treats are next up. They feature the same appeal as Rice Krispies treats but with a colorful, fruity twist. Made with Fruity Pebbles, a bit of Rice Krispies (to balance the sweetness), and lots of marshmallows, this recipe is gooey and sweet and the perfect rainbow treat!

Lightly grease a 9 x 5–inch (23 x 13–cm) loaf pan with butter or cooking spray, then line it with parchment paper, leaving an overhang on the two long sides. Lightly grease the parchment with butter or nonstick cooking spray, then set aside the pan.

Place the butter in a large saucepan, and melt it over medium-low heat. Once it's melted, turn the heat to low, then stir in the salt and vanilla.

Lightly coat a rubber spatula with cooking spray. Working quickly, add 5 ounces (141 g) of the marshmallows, and stir until they are thoroughly melted. Add the Fruity Pebbles and Rice Krispies cereals, and gently fold them in with the prepared spatula until the cereal is completely covered with the marshmallow mixture. Lastly, stir in the remaining 1½ ounces (45 g) of the marshmallows until they are evenly combined (don't worry if they don't melt completely!).

Transfer the mixture to the prepared baking pan. Using the rubber spatula, lightly and gently press the mixture into an even layer. Don't pack the mixture into the pan too tightly, otherwise the treats can end up too dense and will be difficult to bite through! Let the treats stand at room temperature until set, about 45 minutes, before cutting them into bars.

These treats can be stored in an airtight container at room temperature for up to 5 days.

VARIATION TIP: *If you're not a fan of Fruity Pebbles, try Cocoa Pebbles™ for a chocolate version! You can also use all Rice Krispies, for a more classic version!*

PIES & TARTS MADE EASY

Pies and tarts are a staple celebratory food, weekend treat, and sometimes a weeknight meal. They can be sweet, savory, open face, or even handheld. And, while pie making can sometimes seem intimidating, it doesn't have to be! When you break it down, pies and tarts are just a crust and filling. You can dress it up if you want, but even a humble pie is top-notch; even if the crust is imperfect, or the filling runs over the sides, it's the taste of the pie that truly matters.

Whether you're making a pie for a loved one or just to treat yourself, all you need is a good, solid recipe. That's where this chapter comes in. This chapter includes my scaled-down, tried-and-true, best-of-the-best pie and tart recipes. If I had to pick a recipe to eat over and over and over again, it would be the Small-Batch Maple Pecan Tassies (page 109). The slightly tangy cream cheese crust with that perfectly sweetened pecan filling? DROOL. If you're looking to get away with eating dessert for breakfast, I encourage you to try the Strawberry Cardamom Puff Pastry Pop-Tarts® (page 89). And, don't even get me started on the Chocolate Peanut Butter Tartlets (page 102), which are basically like a fancy Reese's peanut butter cup (my favorite candy). Whatever type of pie or tart you're looking to make, and whether you're new to baking or you've been baking for years, this chapter is sure to have something that'll tickle your fancy.

TIPS & TECHNIQUES

SUGAR: Think of the sugar measurements in this chapter more like guidelines than rules. Since the sweetness of fresh fruit can vary, you have to be flexible when working with it. Taste the fruit before you start, and use more or less sugar depending on how sweet it is.

SUBSTITUTIONS: Fruit substitutions are encouraged! Use fresh fruit that's in season and that you like best. Similar fruits, such as different varieties of berries, can be swapped with minimal adjustment. Particularly sweet and juicy fruits, like peaches, may need half the sugar and up to twice the amount of thickener as berries do to keep the filling from becoming too runny.

EGG WASH: Many of the pastry recipes call for an egg wash, made by whisking together an egg and a small amount of water. Brushing the egg wash on the dough gives the baked goods color and gloss. Don't skip this step; it makes all the difference between an Instagram photo that looks just OK and one that pops.

TESTING FOR DONENESS: Use visual cues for doneness; look for bubbly fruit and/or a golden crust. Obviously, fruit pies will need both. For pastries, hand pies, and tarts, look for a golden crust, so you know it's cooked through and perfectly crispy.

STORAGE: Fruit pies and hand pies can be stored loosely covered at room temperature for up to 2 days or in the refrigerator for up to 4 days. The custard pies, hand pies, and tarts, however, should be wrapped and refrigerated and will generally last anywhere from 2 to 5 days, depending on the filling.

FOR THE STRAWBERRY CARDAMOM JAM

16 oz (453 g) strawberries, hulled and coarsely chopped

1½ cups (300 g) granulated sugar

2 tbsp (30 ml) freshly squeezed lemon juice

1 vanilla bean, see Ingredient Tip (page 90)

6 cardamom pods, see Ingredient Tip (page 90)

FOR THE POP-TARTS

2 sheets frozen puff pastry, thawed

Egg wash: 1 large egg + 1 tbsp (15 ml) water

STRAWBERRY CARDAMOM PUFF PASTRY POP-TARTS®

I've had more than my fair share of those silvery packaged (OK . . . I have to admit DRY) crumbly pastry tarts in my day. I would scarf them down for breakfast, a snack, even dinner. Since my boxed Pop-Tart days, however, I've found satisfaction in making everything from scratch. So, naturally, I had to give these classic breakfast treats a major upgrade. The Strawberry Cardamom Jam has the softness and spreading power of jam and the fragrance of heaven, from the sweet/spicy/intense aroma that the vanilla and cardamom give the jam. And, when it's stuffed inside of a buttery, flaky puff pastry? Well, the result is life changing.

They say a sign of maturity is being able to delay pleasure for a greater result; at least, that's what Google told me. So, clearly a sign of maturity is being able to put down that little silver cellophane package, bust out your saucepan, and whip up some homemade strawberry cardamom Pop-Tarts. Man, if only my 18-year-old self could see me now . . .

To make the Strawberry Cardamom Jam, begin by adding the strawberries to the bowl of a blender or food processor. Blend them really well, until they are as smooth as possible, then press the puree through a sieve into a large saucepan. Use a spatula to push the pulp through, leaving the seeds behind. Add the sugar, lemon juice, vanilla bean, and cardamom to the pan, and cook the mixture over medium heat, stirring often. Once the sugar has dissolved, increase the heat to medium-high, and bring the mixture to a rolling boil. Boil the jam for 6 to 7 minutes, or until the jam reaches 220°F (105°C) on an instant-read thermometer. (If you don't have a thermometer, see the Cooking Tip on page 90.)

Once the jam has set, remove the vanilla bean and cardamom pods, and spoon the jam into a clean jar. Cover the jar, and refrigerate it until the jam is completely chilled, about 1 hour.

For the Pop-Tarts, preheat the oven to 375°F (190°C), and line a baking sheet with parchment paper. Unfold the puff pastry sheets, and slice each sheet into six rectangles for a total of twelve. Transfer half of the rectangles onto the prepared baking sheet, and fill them with the jam, leaving a ¼- to ½-inch (6-mm to 1.3-cm) border around the edges; you'll use 1½ to 2 tablespoons (30 to 40 g) of jam per rectangle. Brush the edge with some of the egg wash, and lay a rectangle of puff pastry over the jam. Seal the edges by crimping them with the back of a fork. Repeat these steps until you have six tarts.

(continued)

FOR THE STRAWBERRY GLAZE

1 cup (120 g) powdered sugar

1 tbsp (15 ml) milk

2 tbsp (40 g) Strawberry Cardamom Jam

Using a fork, carefully poke four to five holes into the tops, so steam can vent as they cook. Lightly brush the tarts with the egg wash, and bake them for 20 to 25 minutes, until they are puffed and lightly golden. Remove the tray from the oven and let the tarts cool completely while you make the glaze.

For the glaze, in a medium bowl, whisk together the sugar, milk, and Strawberry Cardamom Jam until the mixture is smooth and the desired consistency is reached. If the glaze is too thick, add more milk or jam. If it's too thin, add more powdered sugar. Drizzle the glaze over the Pop-Tarts and serve them.

These Pop-Tarts are best enjoyed the day they're made, though leftover Pop-Tarts can be stored in an airtight container at room temperature for up to 2 days. This jam isn't processed for long-term storage; any leftover jam should be kept refrigerated and consumed within 2 weeks.

INGREDIENT TIP: *If you don't have any vanilla beans or cardamom pods, you can use 1 teaspoon of vanilla bean paste and 1 teaspoon of ground cardamom in their place.*

COOKING TIP: *If you don't have an instant-read thermometer, you can use the wrinkle test to check if your jam is done. To do this, you'll need to place a ceramic plate in the freezer when you start the recipe. Once your jam has boiled for several minutes, take the pan off the heat and carefully spoon a little jam onto the cold plate. Let it stand for 1 minute, then push the blob of jam with your finger. If the surface of the jam wrinkles, then it has set; if it is still quite runny, then put the pan back on the heat, and boil the jam for another 2 to 4 minutes before testing again.*

FOR THE MIXED BERRY FILLING

3 oz (85 g) fresh raspberries

3 oz (85 g) fresh blackberries

2 oz (56 g) fresh blueberries

2 tbsp (30 ml) freshly squeezed lemon juice

½ cup (100 g) granulated sugar

⅛ tsp fine sea salt

½ tbsp (4 g) cornstarch

FOR THE CRUST, SEE INGREDIENT TIP

1¼ cups (150 g) all-purpose flour

⅛ tsp fine sea salt

1 tbsp (13 g) granulated sugar

½ cup (113 g) unsalted butter, cold and cubed

¼ cup (60 ml) ice water, plus more as needed

Egg wash: 1 large egg + 1 tbsp (15 ml) water

Turbinado sugar, for sprinkling

MINI MIXED BERRY HAND PIES

Here's a dessert where you can mix and match all the berries you want. These mini hand pies are perfect for a small get-together, because, not only are they absolutely adorable, but the bright, fruity flavor completely satisfies even the pickiest eater. The buttery crust is sturdy enough that you don't even need a plate, and they're small enough that you don't need a fork; just eat this pie with your hands. It's OK to lick your fingers when you're done too!

Begin by making the berry filling. Add the raspberries, blackberries, blueberries, lemon juice, sugar, and salt to a medium saucepan. Cook the mixture over medium heat, stirring occasionally, until the mixture comes to a simmer. Continue to cook, occasionally mashing the berries as you stir, until the berries have broken down and released their juices, 6 to 7 minutes. Add the cornstarch and bring the mixture to a rolling boil. Boil the filling for 2 to 3 minutes, or until it's thickened. Transfer the filling to a large bowl to cool completely. Cover the filling with plastic wrap pressed against the surface to prevent a skin from forming.

For the crust, in a medium bowl, whisk together the flour, salt, and sugar to combine. Add the butter, tossing the cubes through the flour until each individual piece is well coated. Working quickly, using a pastry cutter or your fingers, cut the butter into the flour until the butter is about the size of walnut halves.

Make a well in the center of the flour mixture, and add the ice water. Using your hands, toss the flour with the water to start to mix the two together. As the flour begins to hydrate, you can switch to more of a kneading motion—but don't overdo it, or the dough will be tough. Then add more water, about 1 tablespoon (15 ml) at a time, until the dough is properly hydrated. It should be uniformly combined and hold together easily, but it shouldn't look totally smooth. Shape the dough into a disc about 1 inch (2.5 cm) thick, wrap it tightly in plastic wrap, and refrigerate it for at least 1 hour or up to 48 hours.

To assemble the hand pies, line a baking sheet with parchment paper; set aside the pan. On a lightly floured surface, roll out the pie dough until it's about ¼ inch (6 mm) thick. Using a 3-inch (8-cm) round pastry cutter, cut out circles of the pie dough and place them onto the prepared baking sheet; you should have a total of 16 circles. Reroll the dough scraps, if needed.

(continued)

MINI MIXED BERRY HAND PIES (CONTINUED)

Spoon about ½ tablespoon (10 g) of the filling into the center of half of the dough circles. Brush the edges of each circle with the egg wash, and place one of the remaining pieces of dough on top of it. Use a fork to crimp the edges to seal the hand pie. Repeat the process with the remaining dough and jam. Chill the tray of assembled hand pies in the refrigerator for 30 minutes.

Preheat the oven to 400°F (200°C). Brush the chilled hand pies with egg wash (avoid brushing too much on the edges, which will brown more on their own), and sprinkle them generously with the turbinado sugar. Cut a small slash or X in the top of each pie with the tip of a paring knife. Bake the pies for 20 to 25 minutes, until deeply golden brown. Allow them to cool completely before serving. Store leftovers in an airtight container in the refrigerator for up to 3 days. Store any leftover Mixed Berry Filling, tightly covered, in the refrigerator, and use it within 2 weeks.

INGREDIENT TIP: *Making pie crust from scratch can be a little intimidating, so feel free to replace the homemade crust with a store-bought crust if you want! You need only one crust; so just save the second one (if included) for another recipe.*

COOKING TIP: *Make sure to measure the flour correctly. If you don't have a kitchen scale, be sure to use the scoop and sweep method. Use a spoon to scoop the flour into the measuring cup, and then use the flat side of a butter knife to sweep the excess off the top; this way the flour doesn't become compressed when you scoop it out to measure, as too much flour can prevent the dough from coming together.*

FOR THE LEMON CURD

2 large egg yolks

⅓ cup (67 g) granulated sugar

½ tbsp (3 g) lemon zest

2 tbsp + 2 tsp (40 ml) freshly squeezed lemon juice

⅛ tsp fine sea salt

3 tbsp (42 g) unsalted butter, softened

FOR THE TARTS

2 sheets frozen puff pastry, thawed

Egg wash: 1 large egg + 1 tbsp (15 ml) water

24 fresh raspberries

Powdered sugar, for dusting

COOKING TIP: *Use a glass mixing bowl and a silicone whisk for preparing the lemon curd. You want to avoid metal objects, as the high acidity content of lemons can cause the metal to leach into the lemon curd, resulting in an unpleasant metallic flavor.*

LEMON RASPBERRY PUFF PASTRY TARTS

Do you know what happens to puff pastry when it's baked into tart shells? It becomes a tall, flaky skyscraper waiting to be filled with something delicious. Do you know what happens when you put raspberries and lemon curd inside? Magic, my friend. Magic is what happens.

For the curd, in a medium heat-safe glass bowl, combine the egg yolks, sugar, lemon zest, lemon juice, and sea salt. In a saucepan, bring just 2 inches (5 cm) of water to a simmer over medium heat, then set the bowl over the saucepan. Do not let the bottom of the bowl touch the water.

Using a silicone whisk (see the Cooking Tip), whisk the ingredients until they are completely blended, then continue to whisk constantly as the curd cooks. Whisk and cook until the mixture becomes thick, resembling the texture of hollandaise sauce, 9 to 10 minutes. If the curd isn't thickening, turn up the heat and continue constantly whisking.

Remove the pan from the heat. Cut the butter into 3 separate pieces, then whisk the pieces, one at a time, into the curd; the butter will melt from the heat of the curd. Pour the curd into a jar or bowl, and place a piece of plastic wrap directly on it, so it is touching the top of the curd. This prevents a skin from forming on top. The curd will continue to thicken as it cools. Once cool, the plastic wrap can be removed. The curd can be refrigerated for up to 10 days.

Preheat the oven to 400°F (200°C). Line a baking sheet with parchment paper, then set aside the pan.

Working with the first sheet of puff pastry, cut it into thirds, along the lines where the pastry was folded, then stack each piece on top of each other. Using a 3-inch (8-cm) round biscuit cutter, cut out three circles from the stacked puff pastry sheets. Using a 1½-inch (4-cm) round biscuit cutter, cut out inner circles in each stack of pastry rounds, but leave them in place. Repeat with the second sheet of puff pastry so that you have 6 pastry rounds total. Brush each pastry round lightly with the egg wash.

Bake the pastry for 13 to 15 minutes; let it cool completely on the baking sheet. Once cool, cut around the small inner circle of each pastry round with a paring knife and gently push the center down to the base. Fill each tartlet with 1 tablespoon (13 g) of lemon curd, then place two raspberries on top. Cover the raspberries with an additional tablespoon (13 g) of lemon curd, and place two more raspberries on top. Dust the tarts with the powdered sugar.

These puff pastry tarts are best enjoyed on the day they're made. Leftovers can be stored in an airtight container in the refrigerator for up to 2 days.

TOTAL TIME:
1 hour 45 minutes

MAKES: 1 mini galette

FOR THE CRUST, SEE INGREDIENT TIP (PAGE 98)

½ cup + 2 tbsp (75 g) all-purpose flour

⅛ tsp fine sea salt

¼ cup (57 g) unsalted butter, cold and cubed

2 tbsp (30 ml) ice water, plus more as needed

Egg wash: 1 large egg + 1 tbsp (15 ml) water

Turbinado sugar, for sprinkling

FOR THE STRAWBERRY FILLING

9 oz (255 g) fresh strawberries, hulled and sliced

2 tbsp (25 g) granulated sugar

½ tbsp (4 g) cornstarch

½ tsp vanilla extract

Ice cream for serving, optional

STRAWBERRY GALETTE FOR ONE

Galettes are the less-fussy cousins of fruit pies. They're essentially the best of both worlds: all of the deliciousness of a pie with only half the effort. While incredibly easy to make, their appearance is so simple and rustic that it somehow manages to look fancy. The thing I love most about galettes is how customizable they are; in this galette, for example, I used all strawberries, but you could totally opt for a mixture of berries or replace them with a different fruit altogether. Customize it to your liking, and revel in the joy of a few simple ingredients being transformed into something crazy delicious.

For the crust, in a medium bowl, whisk together the flour and salt to combine. Add the butter, tossing the cubes through the flour until each individual piece is well coated. Working quickly, using a pastry cutter or your fingers, cut the butter into the flour until the butter is about the size of walnut halves.

Make a well in the center of the flour mixture, and add the ice water. Using your hands, toss the flour with the water to start to mix the two together. As the flour begins to hydrate, you can switch to more of a kneading motion—but don't overdo it, or the dough will be tough. Then add more water, about 1 tablespoon (15 ml) at a time, until the dough is properly hydrated. It should be uniformly combined and hold together easily, but it shouldn't look totally smooth. Shape the dough into a disc about 1 inch (2.5 cm) thick, wrap it tightly in plastic wrap, and refrigerate it for at least 1 hour or up to 48 hours.

For the filling, in a large bowl, combine the strawberries, sugar, cornstarch, and vanilla. Mix and toss together until the strawberries are evenly coated. Cover the bowl tightly, and let the mixture sit until the dough is ready.

Preheat the oven to 425°F (220°C). Line a large baking sheet with parchment paper. Set aside the pan.

(continued)

STRAWBERRY GALETTE FOR ONE (CONTINUED)

On a lightly floured work surface, roll the dough into a circle (or any shape, really!) about ¼ inch (6 mm) thick. Transfer the dough to the prepared baking sheet. Spoon the berries— but not the juices—into the center of the dough, leaving a 2- to 3-inch (5- to 7.5-cm) border all around. Gently fold the edges of the dough over the fruit, overlapping the dough as necessary. Press gently to seal the edges. Brush the edges with the egg wash, and sprinkle them with the turbinado sugar.

Bake until the filling is bubbly and the crust is golden brown, 28 to 30 minutes. Allow the galette to cool on the baking sheet for 10 minutes before slicing and serving it topped with vanilla ice cream, if using. Leftovers can be stored, covered, at room temperature for up to 2 days, or in the refrigerator for up to 4 days.

INGREDIENT TIP: *Making pie crust from scratch can be a little intimidating, so feel free to replace the homemade crust with a store-bought crust if you want! You need only half of the store-bought crust, so you can either 1) cut the store-bought crust in half and reshape/reroll one half into a circle, saving the other half for later; 2) cut the store-bought crust in half, reshape/reroll both halves into circles and double the filling ingredients to make two galettes; or 3) double the filling ingredients and make a single larger galette.*

TOTAL TIME: 1 hour 45 minutes

MAKES: 4 mini pies

FOR THE CRUST, SEE INGREDIENT TIP (PAGE 101)

1¼ cups (150 g) all-purpose flour

⅛ tsp fine sea salt

1 tbsp (12 g) granulated sugar

½ cup (113 g) unsalted butter, cold and cubed

¼ cup (60 ml) ice water, plus more as needed

Egg wash: 1 large egg + 1 tbsp (15 ml) water

Turbinado sugar, for sprinkling

FOR THE SPICED APPLE FILLING

1 large apple, finely diced (140 g), see Ingredient Tip (page 101)

1 tbsp (15 g) light brown sugar

1 tbsp (12 g) granulated sugar

½ tsp ground cinnamon

⅛ tsp ground nutmeg

⅛ tsp ground cardamom

⅛ tsp fine sea salt

¼ tsp vanilla bean paste

2 tbsp (15 g) all-purpose flour

MINI SPICED APPLE PIES

The best apple pies are often the simplest, and it doesn't get much simpler than this. Finely diced apples are tossed in a mixture of sugar and spices, and then piled into a classic flaky crust. When the mini pies come out of the oven, they're beautiful, golden, and packed full of gooey apple filling. Ice cream on the side is a must, and if you want to grate a little Cheddar cheese over the pies while they're still warm, I won't judge you!

For the crust, in a medium bowl, whisk together the flour, salt, and sugar to combine. Add the butter, tossing the cubes through the flour until each individual piece is well coated. Working quickly, using a pastry cutter or your fingers, cut the butter into the flour until the butter is about the size of walnut halves.

Make a well in the center of the flour mixture, and add the ice water. Using your hands, toss the flour with the water to start to mix the two together. As the flour begins to hydrate, you can switch to more of a kneading motion—but don't overdo it, or the dough will be tough. Then add more water, about 1 tablespoon (15 ml) at a time, until the dough is properly hydrated. It should be uniformly combined and hold together easily, but it shouldn't look totally smooth. Shape the dough into a disc about 1 inch (2.5 cm) thick, wrap it tightly in plastic wrap, and refrigerate it for at least 1 hour or up to 48 hours.

For the filling, in a large bowl, combine the apples, brown sugar, granulated sugar, cinnamon, nutmeg, cardamom, salt, and vanilla bean paste. Mix and toss together until the apple pieces are evenly coated. Cover the bowl tightly and let the mixture sit and macerate until the dough is ready.

Preheat the oven to 400°F (200°C). Lightly spray a 6-cup muffin tin with nonstick cooking spray. Set aside the pan.

On a lightly floured work surface, roll the dough out until it's about ¼ inch (6 mm) thick. Using a 3½-inch (9-cm) round biscuit cutter, cut out eight rounds of the pie crust (rerolling the scraps if necessary), and press half of them into the muffin cups.

(continued)

MINI SPICED APPLE PIES (CONTINUED)

Add the flour to the filling and stir until it's combined. Spoon the apple pieces evenly into each of the dough cups. Add the other four rounds of dough on top, and gently press the edges of the dough together to seal. Brush the tops with the egg wash, and sprinkle them with the turbinado sugar. Bake the mini pies for 23 to 25 minutes, until the filling is bubbling and the crust is deep golden brown. Let the mini pies cool completely before attempting to remove them from the muffin tin.

Leftovers can be stored in an airtight container in the refrigerator for up to 3 days.

INGREDIENT TIP: *Making pie crust from scratch can be a little intimidating so feel free to replace the homemade crust with a store-bought crust if you want! You need only one crust; so just save the second one (if included) for another recipe.*

INGREDIENT TIP: *Selecting the right apples for these mini pies is half the battle, honestly. Generally speaking, you want apples that will hold their shape and not become a mushy mess in the heat of an oven. These types of apples are typically referred to as "baking apples" and include varieties like Braeburn, Honeycrisp, Fuji, Gala, Granny Smith, and Pink Lady. To add depth of flavor to your pies, try mixing a variety of baking apples. My favorite combination is Honeycrisp and Granny Smith!*

FOR THE CHOCOLATE CRUST

1 cup (125 g) all-purpose flour

⅓ cup (40 g) powdered sugar

¼ cup (20 g) unsweetened natural or Dutch-process cocoa powder

¼ tsp fine sea salt

½ cup (113 g) unsalted butter, melted

½ tsp vanilla extract

FOR THE PEANUT BUTTER FILLING

¼ cup (60 ml) heavy cream, cold

2 oz (57 g) cream cheese, softened

¼ cup (30 g) powdered sugar

¼ cup (64 g) creamy peanut butter

¼ tsp vanilla extract

FOR THE TOPPINGS, OPTIONAL

Melted chocolate

Chopped peanuts

Flaky sea salt

MAKE-AHEAD INSTRUC-TIONS: *The tart shells can be baked up to 48 hours in advance. Keep them refrigerated in an air-tight container until you are ready to use them.*

CHOCOLATE PEANUT BUTTER TARTLETS

I love the flavor combination of chocolate and peanut butter, and this tart gives the best of both. A delicious and simple chocolate shortbread-like crust is paired with a creamy, no-bake peanut butter filling. Top it off with a healthy drizzle of melted chocolate, some chopped peanuts, and flaky sea salt, and you have a decadent, upscale version of a Reese's peanut butter cup. It's absolute perfection.

Preheat the oven to 350°F (180°C).

For the crust, in a medium bowl, whisk together the flour, powdered sugar, cocoa powder, and salt. Add the butter and vanilla, and stir together until the dry ingredients are thoroughly moistened. Press the dough evenly along the bottom and sides of three 4.75-inch (12-cm) tart pans with removable bottoms. This recipe makes around 10 ounces (290 g) of dough; use about 3.3 ounces (96 g) in each tart pan.

Place the tart pans on a baking sheet, and bake until the crust looks dry and matte instead of glistening with butter, 15 to 20 minutes. It can be tricky to tell when chocolate doughs are baked enough without burning because the color doesn't change much. The dough will go from glossy to matte and smell lovely and chocolaty when it's baked enough. Check at 15 minutes, and every minute after, until it looks done. Let the crusts cool completely before filling them.

For the filling, in a medium bowl using a hand mixer, beat the heavy cream on medium-high speed for 4 to 5 minutes, until stiff peaks form. To test, when you lift your beater or whisk, peaks will form that will stand straight up and hold their shape. Spoon the whipped cream into a small bowl; set it aside. Using the same mixing bowl (no need to clean it!), beat the cream cheese, powdered sugar, peanut butter, and vanilla together on medium-high speed until the ingredients are well combined. The mixture will be thick. With a silicone spatula, fold in the whipped cream until the mixture is smooth and combined. Be careful not to deflate the cream too much.

Transfer the filling to the tart shells, and smooth the tops with an offset spatula. Chill in the fridge for at least 1 hour, or overnight. For serving, drizzle the tartlets with the melted chocolate, if using, and top them with the peanuts and flaky salt, if using. Cover leftovers and refrigerate them for up to 3 days; you can freeze them for up to 1 month.

VARIATION TIP: *Don't have mini tart pans? No problem! This recipe can also be made as written and will fit into a standard 9-inch (23-cm) tart pan or springform pan.*

TOTAL TIME: 1 hour

MAKES: 2 (6-oz [170-g]) ramekins

FOR THE BLUEBERRY LEMON FILLING

1½ cups (255 g) fresh blueberries, see Ingredient Tip

½ tbsp (3 g) lemon zest, see Ingredient Tip

1 tbsp (15 ml) freshly squeezed lemon juice

2 tbsp (27 g) dark brown sugar

1 tbsp (8 g) cornstarch

FOR THE CRISP TOPPING

½ cup (40 g) old-fashioned oats

¼ cup (30 g) all-purpose flour

¼ cup (55 g) light brown sugar

¼ cup (57 g) unsalted butter, cold and cubed

BLUEBERRY LEMON CRISP FOR TWO

What could be better on a summer day than a fresh blueberry crisp? And, when you add lemon juice and lemon zest to the filling, those wonderful berry flavors shine through even more. This versatile recipe is great with any kind of berry: raspberry, blackberry, strawberry, or a combination! Just use one-and-a-half cups of whatever berries you want, and follow the recipe as directed. Enjoy this crisp hot or cold, with ice cream, with whipped cream, or just by itself.

Preheat the oven to 350°F (180°C), and line a baking sheet with parchment paper.

For the filling, in a medium bowl, combine the blueberries, lemon zest, lemon juice, brown sugar, and cornstarch. Mix and toss until the berries are evenly coated. Divide evenly between two 6-ounce (170-g) oven-safe ramekins.

For the topping, in a large bowl, whisk together the oats, flour, and brown sugar. Using a pastry cutter, a fork, or your fingers, cut the butter into the dry ingredients until the mixture is combined and crumbly. Sprinkle the crumbs evenly over the filling in both ramekins.

Transfer the ramekins to the prepared baking sheet, and bake them for 30 to 35 minutes, or until the topping is golden brown and the fruit juices are bubbling around the edges. Remove the crisps from the oven, place them on a wire rack, and allow them to cool for a few minutes before serving warm. You can also serve them at room temperature or cold.

Store leftovers, tightly covered, in the refrigerator for up to 5 days.

INGREDIENT TIP: *You can use any type of berry in place of blueberries for this dish. To substitute other fruits, such as peaches or apricots, reduce the sugar slightly, unless your fruit is particularly tart.*

INGREDIENT TIP: *The lemon flavor is very present in this crisp; it's not just there as a flavor booster. If you don't like a lot of lemon, omit the zest. The juice alone will help bring out the blueberry flavor without overwhelming it.*

MAKES: 6 mini tarts

MINI PUMPKIN PIE TARTS

For intimate Thanksgiving gatherings or pre-holiday pie cravings, these little pumpkin pie tarts are perfect. This recipe uses sweetened condensed milk to sweeten these adorable mini tarts and help them set up perfectly. It also gives them a rich, smooth texture that is incredibly appealing, not too sweet, and perfectly spiced. You might just find yourself hoarding the leftovers!

FOR THE CRUST

1¼ cups (150 g) all-purpose flour

⅛ tsp fine sea salt

1 tbsp (12 g) granulated sugar

½ cup (113 g) unsalted butter, cold and cubed

¼ cup (60 ml) ice water, plus more as needed

FOR THE PUMPKIN PIE FILLING

½ cup (120 g) pumpkin puree

6 tbsp + 2 tsp (100 g) sweetened condensed milk

½ tsp ground cinnamon

½ tsp pumpkin pie spice

Whipped cream, for serving, optional

For the crust, in a medium bowl, whisk together the flour, salt, and sugar to combine. Add the butter, tossing the cubes through the flour until each individual piece is well coated. Working quickly, using a pastry cutter or your fingers, cut the butter into the flour until the butter is about the size of walnut halves.

Make a well in the center of the flour mixture, and add the ice water. Using your hands, toss the flour with the water and start to mix the two together. As the flour begins to hydrate, you can switch to more of a kneading motion—but don't overdo it, or the dough will be tough. Then add more water, about 1 tablespoon (15 ml) at a time, until the dough is properly hydrated. It should be uniformly combined and hold together easily, but it shouldn't look totally smooth. Shape the dough into a disc about 1 inch (2.5 cm) thick, wrap it tightly in plastic wrap, and refrigerate it for at least 30 minutes or up to 48 hours.

While the crust chills, make the filling. In a medium bowl, whisk together the pumpkin, condensed milk, cinnamon, and pumpkin pie spice until well combined. Place the mixture in the refrigerator until it's needed.

Preheat the oven to 375°F (190°C). Lightly spray a 6-cup muffin tin with nonstick cooking spray. Set aside the pan.

On a lightly floured work surface, roll the dough out until it's about ¼ inch (6 mm) thick. Using a 3½-inch (9-cm) round biscuit cutter, cut out 6 rounds of the pie crust (rerolling the scraps if necessary), and press them into the muffin cups. Evenly spoon the cold filling into each of the cups, filling them to the top. Bake the pies for 22 to 25 minutes, until the center is just about set and the edges are lightly browned. Let the mini pies cool completely before attempting to remove them from the muffin tin. Note: The filling deflates a bit as they cool. Serve the pies at room temperature or refrigerate them and serve cold. Top them with the whipped cream, if using.

Leftovers can be stored in an airtight container in the refrigerator for up to 5 days.

TOTAL TIME:
1 hour 45 minutes

MAKES: 16 pecan tassies

FOR THE CREAM CHEESE CRUST

⅓ cup (76 g) unsalted butter, softened

2 oz (57 g) cream cheese, softened

¾ cup (95 g) all-purpose flour

⅛ tsp fine sea salt

FOR THE MAPLE PECAN FILLING

⅔ cup (80 g) pecan halves

½ cup (110 g) dark brown sugar

2 tbsp + 2 tsp (56 g) pure maple syrup

2 large eggs, room temperature

2 tbsp (28 g) unsalted butter, melted

1 tsp vanilla extract

⅛ tsp fine sea salt

SMALL-BATCH MAPLE PECAN TASSIES

The problem I have with pecan pie is that the deliciously gooey and sweet filling is never juxtaposed with enough flaky crust. Enter pecan tassies. These little pecan pie poppers, with a higher crust-to-filling ratio, offer the perfect bite. I add maple syrup to the filling to both help it set and complement the sweetness. And even you (yes, you) can make this cream cheese crust right 100 percent of the time. The dough is as forgiving as can be. No rolling pin is needed; you just press the dough into mini muffin cups, fill them, and bake. Get ready to win the Thanksgiving dessert game for years to come.

For the crust, in a medium bowl, with a wooden spoon or silicone spatula, or using a handheld mixer, beat the butter and cream cheese together until smooth. Gradually add the flour and salt, and mix until the ingredients are well combined. Wrap the dough in plastic wrap; refrigerate it until it's firm enough to handle, about 1 hour.

For the filling, arrange a rack in the center of the oven, and preheat it to 350°F (180°C). Toast the pecans on a baking sheet in the center of the oven for 5 to 7 minutes, until they are lightly toasted inside; break a few open to check. Let the pecans cool, then finely chop them and set them aside.

In a medium bowl, whisk together the sugar, maple syrup, eggs, butter, vanilla, and salt. Add about half of the chopped pecans, and mix until they are well combined. Separate the chilled dough into 16 even portions, shape them into balls, then press them evenly onto the bottoms and up the sides of the cups of a mini muffin pan. Spoon approximately 1 tablespoon (14 g) of the filling evenly into the prepared shells, filling them all the way to the top. Sprinkle the tassies evenly with the remaining nuts, and bake them for 25 to 27 minutes, or until they are puffed and brown. Remove the pan from the oven, and let the tassies cool for a few minutes in the tin on a wire rack. Remove them from the pan and cool them completely on the wire rack.

Store leftovers in an airtight container at room temperature for up to 2 days.

MAKE-AHEAD INSTRUCTIONS: *The dough can be prepared and stored, well wrapped, in the fridge for up to 3 days or frozen for up to 1 month. Let the dough thaw overnight in the fridge before using it.*

TOTAL TIME: 1 hour

MAKES: 1 (6-inch [15-cm]) cobbler

FOR THE FILLING

1 cup (225 g) sliced peaches, approximately 2 medium peaches

1 tbsp (15 ml) bourbon

2 tbsp (25 g) granulated sugar

1 tbsp (8 g) cornstarch

½ tsp ground cinnamon

⅛ tsp ground nutmeg

2 tbsp (28 g) unsalted butter

FOR THE TOPPING

¾ cup (95 g) all-purpose flour

¼ cup (50 g) granulated sugar

1 tsp baking powder

¼ tsp fine sea salt

6 tbsp (85 g) unsalted butter, cold and cubed

6 tbsp (90 ml) heavy cream

Turbinado sugar, for sprinkling

Cinnamon, for sprinkling

Vanilla ice cream, optional

SKILLET BOURBON PEACH COBBLER FOR TWO

Desserts are immediately 20 times more appealing when served in a mini cast iron skillet, and this little bourbon peach cobbler is no exception. Served with a big scoop of vanilla ice cream, it's the perfect size for two to polish off after dinner. The hint of cinnamon and nutmeg accentuates the peachy flavor perfectly; you'll be dreaming about the buttery cobbler topping for days.

Preheat the oven to 375°F (190°C). To prepare the filling, combine the peaches, bourbon, sugar, cornstarch, cinnamon, and nutmeg in a medium bowl and toss to coat. Set the mixture aside.

For the topping, in a separate medium bowl, sift together the flour, sugar, baking powder, and salt. Add the cubed butter and cut it into the flour with a pastry blender or your hands until the mixture looks like coarse crumbs. Pour in the heavy cream and mix just until the dough comes together, then set it aside in the fridge until it's needed. The dough will be slightly sticky.

Continue making the filling. Line a baking sheet with parchment paper. Melt the butter in a 6-inch (15-cm) cast iron skillet over medium-low heat. Add the peach mixture, and cook it gently until it's heated through, about 5 minutes. Carefully transfer the skillet to the prepared baking sheet (be careful as it'll be hot!). Drop the topping by tablespoonfuls over the warm peaches. Sprinkle the top with the turbinado sugar and a little extra cinnamon, and then bake the cobbler for 30 to 35 minutes, or until the cobbler is browned and the fruit is bubbling. Serve it warm with the ice cream, if using.

VARIATION TIP: *If you prefer not to use alcohol in your baking, just replace the bourbon with vanilla extract!*

WEEKEND BRUNCH

They say there's nothing like a well-balanced, nutritious breakfast to start your day. To which I say, "to heck with that!" From time to time, oatmeal and boring cereal options just don't fulfill your cravings. Besides, breakfast is the best excuse to eat dishes that are practically dessert, all before 10 o'clock in the morning. It's not like your busy schedule won't burn off the calories anyway, right? Right. At least, that's what I tell myself.

Whenever I make breakfast at home on the weekends, I usually lean toward savory dishes: bacon and eggs, biscuits, and the occasional breakfast burrito. But every once in a while, I'm seized by the thought of a slow drizzle of maple syrup bathing a stack of French toast. Or maybe it's a cinnamon roll that comes to mind, with a glistening, sweet cream cheese glaze, or a tall muffin with a sweet crumb topping. The point is, there are just too many delightful treats out there that give you an excuse to eat dessert for breakfast, and (on the weekend especially) that seems like a perfectly reasonable, not to mention delicious, way to start the day. Hey, everything in moderation, including moderation, right . . .

The recipes in this chapter are the ones that I turn to over and over again whenever I need to start my day off with something sweet; their scaled-down portions help me feel a little less guilty. There are the Small-Batch Brown Butter Cinnamon Rolls (page 115) which, thanks to the brown butter, are a tad bit richer and more complex in flavor than your average cinnamon roll. The Chocolate Chip Walnut Banana Muffins (page 125) are really just banana bread in muffin form. The Cereal Milk Baked Doughnuts (page 122) are infinitely customizable and allow you to use whatever your favorite cereal is. I think Fruity Pebbles is the best!

The recipes in this chapter are honestly some of my favorites, and I hope you love them as much as I do. Breakfast? Dessert? I'll let you decide.

TIPS & TECHNIQUES

CORRECT MIXING: You'll have the best success if you follow the mixing instructions closely. "Well combined" means ingredients are mixed until completely incorporated and smooth, while "just combined" means just that: Mix only until you no longer see distinct streaks of one ingredient in the other.

WORKING WITH YEAST: A lot of the recipes in this chapter involve yeast. There are many different kinds of yeast out there, from active dry to instant to rapid rise to fresh. While they all basically do the same thing—get dough to rise—they do it all a little differently. You'll notice that I call for instant yeast every time, which is my preference. However, active dry can be used interchangeably (1:1), you'll just need to activate it in the recipe's warm liquid ingredients instead of mixing it directly into the dry ingredients.

FOR THE BRIOCHE DOUGH

2¼ tsp (7 g) instant dry yeast

½ cup (120 ml) milk, warm (115°F [45°C])

1 large egg, room temperature

2 tbsp (28 g) unsalted butter, melted

2 cups (250 g) all-purpose flour

½ tsp fine sea salt

¼ cup (50 g) granulated sugar

½ tsp vanilla bean paste

FOR THE BROWN BUTTER

½ cup (113 g) unsalted butter, cubed

SMALL-BATCH BROWN BUTTER CINNAMON ROLLS

Craving the perfect morning breakfast treat? These fluffy brown butter cinnamon rolls will surely do the trick. Cinnamon rolls are great because they can be the main meal, served alongside a savory breakfast bake, or simply eaten as a snack. The downside to cinnamon rolls, however, is that they generally only stay fresh for a day or two—which is why making this small-batch version is the perfect solution. Say goodbye to worrying about wasting leftover rolls (because there definitely won't be any).

For the dough, in the bowl of a stand mixer or in a large mixing bowl, mix together the yeast with the milk. Add the egg, butter, flour, salt, sugar, and vanilla bean paste, and mix until the ingredients are just barely combined. Let the mixture stand for 5 minutes, so the flour has time to hydrate.

Using the hook attachment, knead the mixture on medium speed for about 5 minutes, until a soft dough forms. Increase the speed to medium-high, and beat until the dough is soft and supple and pulls away from the sides of the bowl, 8 to 10 minutes. The dough will be very soft, but not overly sticky. Beat in 2 to 4 more tablespoons (15 to 30 g) of flour if the dough seems very sticky; avoid adding more flour than you need. If you do not have a stand mixer with a hook attachment, knead the dough by hand in this step.

Transfer the dough to a lightly floured surface, and knead it with your hands for 1 minute. Form the dough into a ball, and transfer it back to the mixing bowl. Cover the dough loosely with plastic wrap, and let it sit in a warm place until doubled in size, 60 to 90 minutes.

While the dough is rising, brown the butter. Place the butter in a light-colored skillet. (A light-colored skillet will help you determine when the butter begins browning.) Melt the butter over medium heat, stirring constantly. Once melted, the butter will start to foam. Keep stirring. After 5 to 8 minutes, the butter will begin browning; you'll notice lightly browned specks begin to form at the bottom of the pan, and you'll start to smell a nutty aroma. Once the butter is browned, immediately remove it from the heat, pour it into a heat-safe bowl, and put the bowl in the freezer to chill the butter until it's solid. Remove the brown butter from the freezer, and bring it to room temperature, stirring often, until it's soft and spreadable.

(continued)

FOR THE FILLING

¼ cup (55 g) brown butter

½ cup (110 g) dark brown sugar

2 tsp (4 g) ground cinnamon

⅛ tsp fine sea salt

FOR THE CREAM CHEESE ICING

Remaining brown butter

2 oz (57 g) cream cheese, softened

½ cup (60 g) powdered sugar

¼ tsp vanilla bean paste

1 tbsp (15 ml) milk

SMALL-BATCH BROWN BUTTER CINNAMON ROLLS (CONTINUED)

For the filling, in a small bowl, combine the browned butter, brown sugar, cinnamon, and salt. Mix until a paste forms, then set aside the mixture.

Continue to make the rolls. Generously grease the bottom and sides of a 6-cup muffin pan with butter. Turn the risen dough out onto a lightly floured work surface, punch it down, and, using a rolling pin, roll it into a 14 × 6–inch (36 x 15–cm) rectangle. Make sure the dough is smooth and evenly thick.

Spread the filling all over the dough. Starting with the shorter end, tightly roll up the dough to form a 6-inch (15-cm) log; cut the log into 6 even rolls. Arrange them in the prepared muffin cups. Cover the pan, and allow the rolls to rise for 20 to 30 minutes, or until they are nearly doubled in size.

Preheat the oven to 350°F (180°C). Once the rolls have risen, bake them for 25 to 30 minutes, until the rolls are light golden brown and the center of the rolls are cooked through. Remove the pan from the oven, and allow the rolls to cool on a wire rack for about 10 minutes as you make the icing.

For the icing, add the remaining browned butter and the cream cheese to a small bowl, and beat to combine them. Add the powdered sugar, vanilla bean paste, and milk to the bowl, and whisk the icing until it's smooth and combined. If the icing is too thin, add a little more powdered sugar; if it's too thick, add more milk. Drizzle the icing over the warm rolls.

Cover leftover frosted or unfrosted rolls tightly, and store them at room temperature for up to 2 days. Leftover unfrosted rolls can also be frozen for 2 to 3 months. Thaw them overnight in the refrigerator, and warm them up before serving.

MAKE-AHEAD INSTRUCTIONS: *To make the night before serving, prepare the dough, roll, fill, and slice the cinnamon rolls, and place each roll into a muffin cup. Cover the rolls tightly and refrigerate them for a minimum of 8 hours or up to 16 hours. The next morning, remove the rolls from the refrigerator, allow them to rise on the counter for 1 hour, then bake them.*

MAKES: 1 loaf

COOKIES 'N' CREAM BABKA

Most babka recipes yield two loaves minimum, which is great if you're making it for some sort of party or plan on bringing leftovers in to work . . . but for smaller families and those of us who live alone, it's just way too much bread. That's why this Cookies 'n' Cream Babka, which yields only one small loaf, might just be my new favorite thing. Located somewhere between bread and a decadent dessert, this irresistible treat uses the brioche dough from my cinnamon rolls recipe as the base. Then, it's filled with an insanely delicious Cookies 'n' Cream Dark Chocolate Filling, baked until golden brown, and topped with a simple syrup. Babka doesn't get much better than this!

FOR THE BRIOCHE DOUGH

2¼ tsp (7 g) instant dry yeast

½ cup (120 ml) milk, warm (115°F [45°C])

1 large egg, room temperature

3 tbsp (42 g) unsalted butter, melted

2 cups (250 g) all-purpose flour

½ tsp fine sea salt

¼ cup (50 g) granulated sugar

½ tsp vanilla bean paste

FOR THE COOKIES 'N' CREAM DARK CHOCOLATE FILLING

½ cup (113 g) unsalted butter

4 oz (115 g) 70% cacao dark chocolate, chopped

1 tbsp (5 g) black cocoa, see Ingredient Tip (page 118)

1 cup (120 g) powdered sugar

8–10 cream-filled chocolate sandwich cookies, coarsely chopped (I like Oreos®)

For the dough, in the bowl of a stand mixer or in a large mixing bowl, mix together the yeast with the milk. Add the egg, butter, flour, salt, sugar, and vanilla bean paste, and mix until the ingredients are just barely combined. Let the mixture stand for 5 minutes so the flour has time to hydrate.

Using the hook attachment, knead the mixture on medium speed for about 5 minutes, until a soft dough forms. Increase the speed to medium-high, and beat until the dough is soft and supple and pulls away from the sides of the bowl, 8 to 10 minutes. The dough will be very soft, but not overly sticky. Beat in 2 to 4 more tablespoons (15 to 30 g) of flour if the dough seems very sticky; avoid adding more flour than you need. If you do not have a stand mixer with a hook attachment, knead the dough by hand in this step.

Transfer the dough to a lightly floured surface, and knead it with your hands for 1 minute. Form the dough into a ball and transfer it back to the mixing bowl. Cover the dough loosely with plastic wrap, and let it sit in a warm place until doubled in size, 60 to 90 minutes.

While the dough is rising, make the filling. Place the butter and chocolate in a heat-safe bowl. Set it over a pan of gently simmering water to create a double boiler. Stir occasionally, until the chocolate is fully melted. Then, remove the bowl from the heat, and stir in the black cocoa and sugar. Set aside the filling to cool and thicken into a paste.

Grease an 8 x 4–inch (20 x 10–cm) loaf pan, and line it with parchment paper, leaving an overhang on the two long sides, which will help you remove the baked babka later.

(continued)

FOR THE SIMPLE SYRUP

¼ cup (50 g) granulated sugar

¼ cup (60 ml) water

½ tbsp (10 g) honey

⅛ tsp ground cinnamon

COOKIES 'N' CREAM BABKA (CONTINUED)

Turn the risen dough out onto a lightly floured work surface, punch it down, and, using a rolling pin, roll it into a 16 × 12–inch (40 x 30–cm) rectangle. (If the dough resists and contracts when rolling, let it rest for 5 to 10 minutes and then continue rolling.) Make sure the dough is smooth and evenly thick.

Spread the chocolate filling all over the dough, then sprinkle the cookies on top. Starting with the shorter end, tightly roll up the dough to form a 12-inch (30-cm) log. Using a sharp knife, cut the log in half, lengthwise. Turn the dough slightly to ensure the cut sides are facing upwards on both pieces. Pinch the ends together on one side, then gently twist the two pieces of dough, pinching the other ends together as well. Carefully push on both ends to compress the twisted strands of dough until they are about the length of your loaf pan. Using both hands, carefully place the babka into the prepared loaf pan, tucking the ends under slightly if needed. Cover and let proof somewhere warm for 45 to 60 minutes, or until risen and puffy.

While the loaf is proofing, preheat the oven to 350°F (180°C).

Once risen, put the loaf pan on a baking sheet, and bake the babka for 40 to 45 minutes, until the babka is a deep, golden brown and measures 190°F (90°C) on an instant-read thermometer.

Make the simple syrup while the babka is baking. In a small saucepan, bring the sugar, water, honey, and cinnamon to a boil. Let the mixture boil for 2 to 3 minutes, or until the sugar is completely dissolved. Remove the syrup from the heat and let it stand.

Remove the babka from the oven, and immediately brush the loaf with the sugar syrup. Cool the babka in the pan for 15 minutes, then remove it to a wire rack. Allow it to cool completely before slicing it.

Store leftovers in an airtight container for up to 3 days. Leftovers can also be frozen for 2 to 3 months. Thaw the babka overnight in the refrigerator and warm it up before serving.

MAKE-AHEAD INSTRUCTIONS: *To make the babka the night before serving, prepare the dough, roll, fill, and shape the babka, and place it into the prepared loaf pan. Cover the babka tightly, and refrigerate it for for a minimum of 8 hours or up to 16 hours. The next morning, remove the pan from the refrigerator and allow the babka to rise on the counter for 1 to 2 hours before baking it.*

INGREDIENT TIP: *Black cocoa is an ultra-Dutch processed cocoa powder, meaning all of the acidity has been neutralized. The result is a cocoa powder that's completely mellow, non-bitter, and very black (think Oreo cookies). You can replace the black cocoa with an equal amount of regular or Dutch-processed cocoa, if that's all you have on hand. However, the final taste of the filling, while still delicious, will be a little different.*

PUMPKIN CRUMB CAKE MUFFINS

There's just something about brown butter that makes everything taste better. These Pumpkin Crumb Cake Muffins are no exception. The fluffy and moist muffins are loaded with pumpkin and warm spices, and then topped with a Brown Butter Pumpkin Spice Crumb Topping. Are they as delicious as they sound? ABSOLUTELY! They're basically autumn in a muffin pan—one bite and you'll be dreaming of crisp fall days, pumpkin spice lattes, and big slouchy sweaters.

FOR THE BROWN BUTTER PUMPKIN SPICE CRUMB TOPPING

¼ cup (57 g) unsalted butter, cubed

1½ tbsp (25 g) dark brown sugar

1½ tbsp (18 g) granulated sugar

½ tsp pumpkin pie spice, see Ingredient Tip

⅛ tsp fine sea salt

½ cup (60 g) all-purpose flour

FOR THE PUMPKIN MUFFINS

1 cup (120 g) all-purpose flour

½ tsp baking powder

¼ tsp baking soda

¼ tsp fine sea salt

1½ tsp (3 g) pumpkin pie spice, see Ingredient Tip

½ cup (100 g) granulated sugar

¼ cup (55 g) light brown sugar

¼ cup (60 ml) vegetable oil

¾ cup (185 g) pumpkin puree

Preheat the oven to 425°F (220°C). Spray a 6-cup muffin pan with nonstick spray or line it with cupcake liners, then set it aside.

For the crumb topping, begin by browning the butter. Place the butter in a light-colored skillet. (A light-colored skillet will help you determine when the butter begins browning.) Melt the butter over medium heat, stirring constantly. Once it's melted, the butter will start to foam. Keep stirring. After 5 to 8 minutes, the butter will begin browning; you'll notice lightly browned specks begin to form at the bottom of the pan, and you'll start to smell a nutty aroma. Once the butter is browned, immediately remove it from the heat, and pour it into a heat-safe bowl.

Add the dark brown sugar, granulated sugar, pumpkin pie spice, and salt to the brown butter. Stir until the ingredients are evenly combined. Add in the flour, and mix with a fork until the flour is completely incorporated. Transfer the bowl to the fridge until you are ready to use the topping.

For the muffins, in a medium bowl, whisk together the flour, baking powder, baking soda, salt, and pumpkin pie spice until the ingredients are combined, then set aside the mixture. In a separate medium bowl, whisk the granulated sugar, brown sugar, oil, and pumpkin puree together until they are combined. Pour the dry ingredients into the wet ingredients, then fold everything together gently until just combined and no flour pockets remain.

Spoon the batter into the prepared muffin pan, filling each cup almost full; you'll use 4 to 4½ tablespoons (90 g) of batter per cup. Take the crumb topping out of the fridge. Evenly sprinkle the mixture on top of the muffin batter. After adding the crumb topping, gently press the crumbs down into the batter so they stick when the muffins rise in the oven.

Bake the muffins for 5 minutes. Keeping the muffins in the oven, reduce the oven temperature to 350°F (180°C), and bake them for 15 to 17 minutes, or until a toothpick inserted into the center comes out clean. Allow the muffins to cool for 10 minutes in the pan before removing them to a wire rack to cool completely.

Cover leftover muffins tightly, and store them at room temperature for 1 to 2 days or in the refrigerator for up to 1 week.

INGREDIENT TIP: *If you don't have pumpkin pie spice, you can use ⅛ teaspoon each of cinnamon, nutmeg, ginger, and cloves for the crumb topping and 1 teaspoon cinnamon, ¼ teaspoon nutmeg, and ⅛ teaspoon each of ginger and cloves for the muffins.*

TOTAL TIME: 40 minutes

MAKES: 6–8 doughnuts

FOR THE CEREAL MILK DOUGHNUTS

½ cup of your favorite cereal

¾ cup (180 ml) milk

2 tbsp (28 g) unsalted butter, melted

¼ cup (50 g) granulated sugar

1 large egg, room temperature

2 tbsp (30 g) sour cream, room temperature

½ tsp vanilla extract

1 cup (125 g) all-purpose flour

½ tsp baking powder

½ tsp baking soda

¼ tsp fine sea salt

FOR THE CEREAL MILK GLAZE

½ cup (60 g) powdered sugar

2 tbsp (30 ml) cereal milk

¼ cup your favorite cereal, optional

CEREAL MILK BAKED DOUGHNUTS

These doughnuts are incredibly soft and moist and incorporate your favorite cereal milk into both the batter and the glaze! Hello childhood brunch goals! Growing up, Fruity Pebbles™ and Froot Loops® were always my go-to cereals of choice; and they still kind of are . . . They're crunchy, fruity (read: sugary), and absolutely delicious. If you're not a Fruity Pebbles or Froot Loops fan (and if so, I don't even wanna know you exist), you can substitute any kind of cereal in its place. Cap'N Crunch®? Check! Lucky Charms™? Yup! Cinnamon Toast Crunch™? Totally! I've tried them all and they were unreal! Whatever cereal you have on hand should work. So, customize these doughnuts to your heart's content and enjoy what I'm sure will be delicious results every single time.

Preheat the oven to 350°F (180°C). Spray a doughnut pan with nonstick cooking spray; set aside the pan.

For the doughnuts, in a small bowl, soak the cereal of your choice in the milk for 15 minutes. Strain the milk through a fine-mesh sieve into a small glass measuring cup. In a medium bowl, whisk together the butter, sugar, egg, sour cream, vanilla, and ½ cup (120 ml) of the cereal milk until the ingredients are well combined; set aside the mixing bowl. Reserve the remaining cereal milk for the glaze, and set it aside.

In a large bowl, whisk together the flour, baking powder, baking soda, and salt. Pour the wet ingredients into the dry ingredients, and mix until they are just combined. The batter will be slightly thick. Spoon the batter into a large resealable plastic bag or pastry bag, and pipe it into the doughnut cavities, filling them about two-thirds of the way full.

Bake the doughnuts for 8 to 10 minutes, or until the edges and tops are lightly browned. To test, poke your finger into the top of the doughnut. If the doughnut bounces back, they're done. Cool the doughnuts in the pan for 1 to 2 minutes, then transfer them to a wire rack to cool completely. Regrease the doughnut pan and bake any remaining doughnut batter.

Make the glaze while the doughnuts cool. Whisk together the powdered sugar and 2 tablespoons (30 ml) of the reserved cereal milk until they are fully combined. If the glaze is too thin, add a little more powdered sugar; if it's too thick, add more cereal milk. Dip each doughnut into the glaze and set it glaze-side up on a cooling rack. Immediately sprinkle the doughnuts with bits of your favorite cereal, if using.

The doughnuts are best served immediately. Leftovers keep well, covered tightly, at room temperature for up to 1 day.

TOTAL TIME: 45 minutes

MAKES: 4 muffins

½ cup (60 g) all-purpose flour

¼ tsp ground cinnamon

¼ tsp baking powder

¼ tsp baking soda

⅛ tsp fine sea salt

2 tbsp (28 g) unsalted butter, melted

¼ cup (50 g) granulated sugar

3 tbsp (42 g) light brown sugar

⅓ cup (85 g) mashed banana, approximately 1 large banana

1 tbsp (15 g) applesauce

½ tsp vanilla extract

¼ cup (44 g) semisweet chocolate chips

¼ cup (30 g) chopped walnuts

Turbinado sugar, for topping

CHOCOLATE CHIP WALNUT BANANA MUFFINS

There's no better use for overripe bananas than a batch of banana bread. And, this recipe is basically just banana bread in muffin form. It's so good it'll have you forgetting to eat that last banana or two in the bunch just for an excuse to make it. Lightly spiced with cinnamon and loaded with chocolate chips and walnuts, it's not just another banana bread muffin variation, it's THE banana bread muffin variation.

Preheat the oven to 375°F (190°C). Spray a 6-cup muffin pan with nonstick spray or line it with cupcake liners, then set it aside.

In a medium bowl, whisk together the flour, cinnamon, baking powder, baking soda, and salt until combined, then set aside the mixture. In a separate medium bowl, whisk the butter, granulated sugar, brown sugar, banana, applesauce, and vanilla together until well combined. Pour the dry ingredients into the wet ingredients, add the chocolate chips and walnuts, then fold everything together gently just until the ingredients are combined and no flour pockets remain.

Spoon the batter into the prepared muffin pan, filling the cups almost full; you'll use 4 to 4½ tablespoons (85 g) of batter per cup. Top the muffins with the turbinado sugar, and bake them for 20 to 22 minutes, or until a toothpick inserted into the center comes out clean. Allow the muffins to cool for 10 minutes in the muffin pan before removing them to a wire rack to cool completely.

Cover leftover muffins tightly, and store them at room temperature for 1 to 2 days or in the refrigerator for up to 5 days.

FOR THE BRIOCHE DOUGH

½ cup (120 ml) milk, warm (115°F [45°C])

2 tbsp (25 g) granulated sugar

2¼ tsp (7 g) instant dry yeast

1 large egg, room temperature

½ tsp vanilla bean paste

½ tsp fine sea salt

2¼ cups (280 g) all-purpose flour

¼ cup (57 g) unsalted butter, softened, divided

Canola or vegetable oil, for frying

SMALL-BATCH BRIOCHE DOUGHNUTS

If you want a doughnut in the morning, there are plenty of stores that will sell you one. However, no doughnut will taste as good as one you've made yourself. I usually put it off because I think it'll be too much work . . . but then I make them, and I wonder why I don't make homemade doughnuts all the time, because they're the BEST (and easier than you might expect). What's even better is that they're infinitely customizable. Need a simple finish? Toss them in powdered sugar or cinnamon sugar. Looking to dress them up? Try a glaze—a thin glaze for an all-over coating, or a thicker glaze, my favorite, for that perfect doughnut-shop look. Regardless of what you decide, you're in for a serious treat!

For the dough, in the bowl of a stand mixer, mix together the milk, sugar, and yeast. Add the egg, vanilla bean paste, salt, and flour, and mix until the ingredients are just barely combined and a shaggy dough forms.

Using the hook attachment, beat the mixture on medium speed for about 5 minutes, until a soft dough forms. With the mixer running slowly, add in the butter, 1 tablespoon (14 g) at a time, working it into the dough. Knead the dough for 10 to 15 minutes, or until the dough is smooth and elastic and pulling away from the sides of the bowl. (The dough may separate and fall apart when adding the butter, but it will come together as you continue kneading.)

Transfer the dough to a lightly floured surface, and knead it with your hands for 1 minute. Form the dough into a ball and transfer it back to the greased bowl. Cover the dough loosely with plastic wrap, and let it sit in a warm place until doubled in size, 60 to 90 minutes.

Turn the dough out onto a well-floured surface, and roll the dough out to about ½ inch (1.3 cm) thick. Using a 3-inch (8-cm) round pastry cutter, cut out circles of dough, and place them on a parchment paper–lined baking sheet, leaving room between each one. Cut holes from the middles of the circles, using a 1-inch (2.5-cm) pastry cutter. Place the doughnut holes on the sheet to proof alongside the doughnuts. Cut the remainder of the dough into doughnut holes (you can reroll and cut additional doughnuts if you want, but they will not be as neat). Then, cover the baking sheet with plastic wrap.

Allow the doughnuts to proof for 20 minutes (this will take longer if your kitchen is cold, but check after 20 minutes to see how they are doing). To test if the doughnuts are done proofing, poke them lightly with your finger; it should leave a slight indentation.

(continued)

1 cup (120 g) powdered sugar

3½ tbsp (52 ml) milk

1 tsp vanilla bean paste

SMALL-BATCH BRIOCHE DOUGHNUTS (CONTINUED)

While the doughnuts are proofing, heat the oil to 350°F (180°C) in a deep fryer or a large heavy-bottomed pot (cast iron works great). Line a baking sheet with a double layer of paper towels for draining the doughnuts.

Once the oil has come to temperature, gently lower the doughnuts, no more than two to three at a time, into the hot oil. Fry until the doughnuts are golden brown on the underside, 2 to 3 minutes. Carefully turn the doughnuts over, and fry them for 2 to 3 minutes, or until the other side is golden brown as well. Using a slotted spoon, remove the doughnuts to the paper towel–lined baking sheet to remove any excess oil, and then transfer them to a cooling rack to cool completely before glazing. Repeat the frying process with the rest of the doughnuts.

To make the glaze, whisk together the sugar and milk until well combined and smooth. Add the vanilla bean paste and whisk until it's evenly incorporated. If the glaze is too thin, add a little more powdered sugar; if it's too thick, add more milk. Dip each doughnut into the glaze and place, glaze-side up, on a cooling rack until the glaze is fully set.

VARIATION TIP: *Try one of the following variations, or come up with your own!*

STRAWBERRY GLAZE: *In a food processor, process 1 cup (120 g) of powdered sugar and ½ cup (10 g) of freeze-dried strawberries. Transfer the mixture to a bowl and add 3 tablespoons (45 ml) of milk and ½ teaspoon of vanilla extract, mixing until smooth.*

ORANGE GLAZE: *Mix 1 cup (120 g) of powdered sugar, 1 tablespoon (5 g) of orange zest, and 3 tablespoons (45 ml) of freshly squeezed orange juice until smooth.*

CINNAMON SUGAR: *Whisk together 1 cup (200 g) of granulated sugar and 1 tablespoon (6 g) of ground cinnamon; toss the doughnuts in the cinnamon mixture while they're still warm.*

MAKE-AHEAD INSTRUCTIONS: *To make the night before serving, prepare the dough and cover the bowl tightly with plastic wrap. Refrigerate for a minimum of 8 hours or up to 16 hours. The next morning, remove the dough from the refrigerator, and proceed with rolling and cutting the doughnuts. Note that the doughnuts will take 10 to 20 minutes longer to proof due to the cold dough.*

TOTAL TIME: 3 hours

MAKES: 4 bagels

FOR THE BAGELS

1⅓ cups (169 g) bread flour

2¼ tsp (7 g) instant dry yeast

1 tsp fine sea salt

¼ tsp ground cinnamon

1 tbsp + 1 tsp (28 g) honey

½ cup (120 ml) water, warm (115°F [45°C])

FOR THE CINNAMON CRUNCH TOPPING

¼ cup (55 g) dark brown sugar

2 tbsp (25 g) granulated sugar

½ tbsp (3 g) ground cinnamon

2 tbsp (28 g) unsalted butter, melted and divided

CINNAMON CRUNCH BAGELS

Growing up, one of my absolute favorite treats was a warm cinnamon crunch bagel from Panera Bread. Now I'll admit, I haven't had a Panera bagel in a loooooong time, so I can't state with certainty that these are a good copycat recipe. That said, these are absolutely, ridiculously, outrageously good bagels. And, they have such a nostalgic taste. So, in my book . . . they're just perfection. The crunchy topping is amazing, and the bagel itself is dense and chewy, just the way bagels should be!

For the bagels, in the bowl of a stand mixer or in a large mixing bowl, whisk together the flour, yeast, salt, and cinnamon. Add the honey and water, and mix until the ingredients are just barely combined. Let the mixture stand for 5 minutes so the flour has time to hydrate.

Using the hook attachment, knead the mixture on medium speed for about 5 minutes until a soft dough forms. Increase the speed to medium-high, and beat until the dough is soft and supple and pulls away from the sides of the bowl, about 5 minutes. The dough will be very soft, but not overly sticky. Beat in 1 to 2 more tablespoons (8 to 15 g) of flour if the dough seems very sticky; avoid adding more flour than you need. If you do not have a stand mixer with a hook attachment, knead the dough by hand in this step.

Transfer the dough to a lightly floured surface, and knead it with your hands for 1 minute. Form the dough into a ball, then transfer it back to the mixing bowl. Cover the dough loosely with plastic wrap, and let it sit in a warm place until doubled in size, 45 to 60 minutes.

While the dough is rising, prepare the topping. In a small bowl, whisk together the dark brown sugar, granulated sugar, and cinnamon. Add 1 tablespoon (14 g) of the melted butter to the sugar mixture, and stir with a fork until the mixture resembles wet sand. Set aside the mixture.

Line a baking sheet with parchment paper or a silicone baking mat. If using parchment paper, lightly spray it with nonstick spray or grease it with butter. Set aside the pan.

When the dough is ready, punch it down to release any air bubbles. Divide the dough into four equal pieces, and shape each piece into a ball. Press your index finger through the center of each ball to make a hole about 2 inches (5 cm) in diameter. Arrange the bagels on the prepared baking sheet, and allow them to rise, uncovered, at room temperature for 20 minutes, then transfer them to the fridge for 10 to 15 minutes.

(continued)

FOR THE BAKING SODA BATH

1 cup (240 ml) water

2 tsp (10 g) baking soda

CINNAMON CRUNCH BAGELS (CONTINUED)

While the bagels rise, preheat the oven to 400°F (200°C), and prepare the baking soda bath.

For the bath, bring the water and baking soda to a boil in a large pot. Once the bagels have risen, remove them from the fridge, and, working with one bagel at a time, drop the bagel into the boiling water for 20 to 30 seconds. (Any more than that and your bagels will have a metallic taste, so be careful!) Using a slotted spatula, lift the bagel out of the water and allow as much of the excess water to drip off as possible. Place the bagel back onto the prepared baking sheet, and brush it with some of the remaining melted butter, then sprinkle it with the Cinnamon Crunch Topping. Repeat with the remaining bagels.

Bake the bagels for 15 to 17 minutes, or until golden brown. Remove them from the oven, and allow the bagels to cool on the baking sheets for 20 minutes, then transfer them to a wire rack to cool completely.

Slice, toast, and top with whatever you want! Cover leftover bagels tightly, and store them at room temperature for up to 2 days.

MAPLE BACON SCONES

The addictive nature of these scones might sneak up on you, even if you're someone who doesn't normally appreciate sweet and savory combinations. At first bite, you get a burst of sweet Maple Glaze, but it doesn't take long before the salty, smoky taste of bacon comes out to play, and suddenly there's a maple bacon party going on in your mouth, and you're not sure you ever want it to stop.

FOR THE SCONES

1½ cups (180 g) all-purpose flour

2 tbsp (25 g) granulated sugar

½ tbsp (8 g) baking powder

¼ tsp baking soda

½ tsp fine sea salt

¼ cup (57 g) unsalted butter, cold and cubed

2 tbsp (30 g) applesauce

¼ cup (60 ml) milk, plus more as needed

½ tsp maple extract, optional

1 cup (70 g) diced cooked bacon, see Ingredient Tip

1 tbsp (15 ml) heavy cream

Turbinado sugar, for sprinkling

FOR THE MAPLE GLAZE

1 tbsp (15 g) unsalted butter

2 tbsp (40 g) pure maple syrup

½ cup (60 g) powdered sugar

For the scones, line a baking sheet with parchment paper. In a medium bowl, combine the flour, sugar, baking powder, baking soda, and salt. Add the butter and, using a pastry cutter or your fingers, work it in until the mixture is crumbly. In a small bowl, whisk together the applesauce, milk, and maple extract, if using. Add the wet ingredients to the dry ingredients, along with the bacon. Mix just until everything is evenly moistened.

Pour the dough onto the counter and, with floured hands, work the dough into a ball as best you can. The dough will be sticky! If it's too sticky, add a little more flour. If it seems too dry, add 1 to 2 more tablespoons (15 to 30 ml) of milk. Press the dough into a disc about ½ inch (1.3 cm) thick and, with a sharp knife or bench scraper, cut the dough into 6 wedges.

Place the scones on the prepared baking sheet about 2 inches (5 cm) apart and refrigerate them for 15 minutes. Meanwhile, preheat the oven to 425°F (220°C).

Brush the scones with the heavy cream, and sprinkle the tops with the turbinado sugar. Bake the scones for 18 to 20 minutes, or until they are golden brown around the edges and on top. Remove them from the oven and let them cool for a few minutes.

To make the maple glaze, combine the butter and maple syrup in a small saucepan over medium heat, and stir until combined. Remove the saucepan from the heat and stir in the powdered sugar until the mixture is smooth. Immediately drizzle the glaze onto the scones.

Leftover scones keep well at room temperature for 2 days or in the refrigerator for 5 days.

INGREDIENT TIP: *My favorite no-fuss way to cook bacon is to bake it in the oven for 15 to 20 minutes at 400°F (200°C) on an aluminum foil–lined baking sheet. Just be sure to remove the bacon and place it on a paper towel–lined plate when it's cooked; gently pat the excess grease on top dry so the bacon can crisp up. This method makes cleanup quick and easy and means you don't have to stand over the bacon while it cooks.*

PUMPKIN CRULLERS

Looking for a pumpkin dessert but not quite ready to go full-on pumpkin pie yet? These pumpkin crullers might be just the thing. They're made with pâte à choux (aka choux pastry), which means the only leavener is steam, as opposed to yeast, baking soda, or baking powder. The result is a perfectly crisp doughnut that is lighter than air, with all sorts of nooks and crannies to hold onto the Pumpkin Spice Sugar topping.

FOR THE CRULLERS

⅓ cup + 2 tsp (90 ml) water

¼ cup (57 g) unsalted butter

½ cup (120 g) pumpkin puree

¼ tsp fine sea salt

¾ cup (90 g) all-purpose flour

¼ tsp pumpkin pie spice

3 large eggs, plus one extra whisked egg, if needed

Canola oil, for frying

FOR THE PUMPKIN SPICE SUGAR

¼ cup (50 g) granulated sugar

½ tsp pumpkin pie spice

Cut parchment paper into six 5 x 5–inch (13 x 13–cm) squares; set them aside.

For the crullers, place the water and butter in a medium saucepan over medium-high heat, and stir until the butter is completely melted. Stir in the pumpkin puree and salt, and cook over medium-high heat for 1 to 2 minutes. Remove the pan from the heat and add the flour and pumpkin pie spice, stirring with a wooden spoon until the flour is completely incorporated.

Place the pan back over medium heat. Continue to cook and stir for 1 to 2 minutes to steam away as much water as possible. The more moisture you can remove, the lighter your pastry will be.

Move the mixture to the bowl of a stand mixer fitted with the paddle attachment. Mix for 1 to 2 minutes to allow it to cool. Then mix on medium speed and add the first egg. Let it mix in completely, then scrape down the sides of the bowl.

Add the second and third eggs, one at a time, and mix them in completely, until the paste becomes smooth and glossy. If the consistency is right, when you pull the paddle up, the dough sticking to the paddle should hang down in a V-shape ribbon that slowly breaks off. If your batter isn't the right consistency, add some of the whisked egg. Once your dough is the right consistency, transfer the batter to a piping bag fitted with a large open star tip.

Pipe 3½-inch (9-cm) diameter circles onto the parchment paper squares, ending each with a little flick of your wrist. Place the squares on a baking sheet.

Heat at least 2 inches (5 cm) of oil in a heavy-bottomed pot until a thermometer registers 360 to 370°F (180 to 190°C).

Mix the Pumpkin Spice Sugar while the oil is heating up; whisk the sugar and pumpkin pie spice together in a small bowl.

Working in batches, place two crullers at a time into the oil, paper-side up. Remove the parchment paper with tongs. Fry the crullers on each side until golden brown, 3 to 4 minutes. Remove the crullers with tongs, and drain them briefly on a paper towel–lined plate, then toss each cruller in the sugar mixture. Repeat with the rest of the piped crullers.

Crullers are best on the day they're made; however, you can store them in an airtight container at room temperature for 1 day.

MAKES: 4–6 waffles

6 tbsp (90 ml) milk, warm (115°F [45°C])

2¼ tsp (7 g) instant dry yeast

1 tbsp (15 g) light brown sugar

1 large egg, room temperature

½ cup (113 g) unsalted butter, melted

1¾ cups (210 g) all-purpose flour

½ tsp fine sea salt

1 tsp vanilla extract

4 oz (115 g) pearl sugar, see Ingredient Tip

BELGIAN LIEGE WAFFLES

These rich Belgian liege waffles take a bit of planning compared to basic waffles, but one bite and you'll forgive the extra time they take and the giant mess they leave on your waffle iron. With their buttery brioche consistency and pockets of sweet, sticky sugar throughout, they're decidedly more dessert than breakfast.

In the bowl of a stand mixer or in a large mixing bowl, mix together the milk and yeast. Add the brown sugar, egg, butter, flour, salt, and vanilla, and mix until the ingredients are just barely combined. Let the mixture stand for 5 minutes so the flour has time to hydrate.

Using the hook attachment, knead the mixture on medium speed for about 5 minutes, until a soft dough forms that pulls away from the sides of the bowl. The dough will be very soft and glossy, but not overly sticky. If you do not have a stand mixer with a hook attachment, knead the dough by hand in this step. Form the dough into a ball and transfer it back to the bowl. Cover the dough loosely with plastic wrap, and let it sit in a warm place to rise until it's just about doubled in size, about 45 minutes.

After the dough has risen, fold in the pearl sugar with either a spatula or your hands until it's evenly dispersed. Weigh the dough, and divide it into four equal pieces. This recipe makes around 20 ounces (565 g) of dough; each piece of dough will weigh approximately 5 ounces (141 g). Place the dough in the refrigerator until it's needed.

Heat your waffle iron according to the manufacturer's instructions. Working with one or two balls of dough at a time (leave the rest in the refrigerator), arrange the dough on the waffle iron, and cook until it's golden brown all over, 2 to 5 minutes depending on your iron. Use tongs to transfer the waffles to a baking sheet or cooling rack. Some of the sugar will melt out of the waffles and collect in your iron, adding an extra layer of glossy molten sugar to each waffle as you continue to cook them. Serve the waffles warm.

Leftovers can be stored in an airtight container at room temperature for up to 2 days.

INGREDIENT TIP: *You can find Belgian pearl sugar online or in craft bake shops. To make your own pearl sugar, combine 1½ cups (300 g) of granulated sugar and 2 tablespoons (30 ml) of water in a large saucepan and stir it so that the sugar clumps into small bits. Cook over very low heat, stirring occasionally, 25 to 30 minutes. The sugar should dry out but not caramelize. Pour the sugar onto a plate and let it cool. Break up any large clumps with your fingers, and sift through to collect ¾ cup (115 g) of pea-sized clumps, leaving smaller sugar granules behind. Making the pearl sugar this way will produce more than is required for the waffles, but the only way to get enough large clumps is to start with more sugar than you need.*

FOR THE BRIOCHE DOUGH

¾ cup (95 g) all-purpose flour

2¼ tsp (7 g) instant dry yeast

1 tbsp (13 g) granulated sugar

½ tsp fine sea salt

¼ cup (60 ml) milk, warm (115°F [45°C])

1 tbsp + 1 tsp (20 ml) water, warm (115°F [45°C])

1 tbsp (14 g) unsalted butter, melted

FOR THE CINNAMON SUGAR COATING

¼ cup (55 g) dark brown sugar

½ tsp ground cinnamon

3 tbsp (42 g) unsalted butter, melted

FOR THE VANILLA GLAZE

½ cup (60 g) powdered sugar

1 tbsp (15 ml) milk

¼ tsp vanilla bean paste

SMALL-BATCH MONKEY BREAD MUFFINS

Here is a completely homemade monkey bread recipe in muffin form. Brioche dough is rolled into balls, dipped in melted butter and cinnamon sugar, then baked until bubbling, and glazed to perfection. This is perfect for dessert, any holiday breakfast, or weekend brunch.

For the dough, in the bowl of a stand mixer or in a large mixing bowl, whisk together the flour, yeast, sugar, and salt. Add the milk, water, and butter, and mix until the ingredients are just barely combined. Let the mixture stand for 5 minutes so the flour has time to hydrate.

Using the hook attachment, knead the mixture on medium speed for about 5 minutes, until a soft dough forms. Increase the speed to medium-high, and beat until the dough is soft and supple and pulls away from the sides of the bowl, about 5 minutes. The dough will be very soft, but not overly sticky. Beat in 1 to 2 more tablespoons (8 to 15 g) of flour if the dough seems very sticky; avoid adding more flour than you need. If you do not have a stand mixer with a hook attachment, knead the dough by hand in this step.

Transfer the dough to a lightly floured surface, and knead it with your hands for 1 minute. Form the dough into a ball, then transfer it back to the mixing bowl. Cover the dough loosely with plastic wrap, and let it sit in a warm place until doubled in size, 45 to 60 minutes.

While the dough is rising, prepare the coating. In a small bowl, whisk together the brown sugar and cinnamon. Place the melted butter in a separate small bowl and set it aside. Spray a 6-cup muffin pan with nonstick spray or line it with cupcake liners and set it aside.

Gently remove the dough from the bowl and pat into a rough 9 x 5–inch (23 x 13–cm) rectangle. Using a bench scraper or knife, cut the dough into 32 pieces. Roll each dough piece into a ball. Working with one at a time, dip the balls into the melted butter, allowing excess butter to drip back into the bowl. Roll each ball in the cinnamon sugar mixture, then layer five to six dough balls into each muffin cup. Cover the pan with plastic wrap, and let the muffins proof for 30 to 45 minutes, or until they are risen and puffy.

Preheat the oven to 350°F (180°C). Once risen, put the muffin pan on a baking sheet, and bake the muffins for 30 to 33 minutes, until they're golden brown and measure 190°F (90°C) on an instant-read thermometer.

Prepare the vanilla glaze. In a small bowl, whisk together the sugar, milk, and vanilla bean paste until smooth. Drizzle the glaze over the warm muffins.

These muffins are best served on the day they're prepared. Any leftovers should be stored, covered tightly with plastic wrap, at room temperature or in the refrigerator for up to 2 days.

SAVORY TREATS

I'm not knocking sweet treats, but who doesn't also like indulging in fresh-from-the-oven savory baked goods? If savory items are more your thing, then this is definitely the chapter for you. Say "baking" or "baked goods" to someone and visions of cakes, cookies, and brownies are sure to come to mind. Savory baking shouldn't be underestimated, though!

Baked wonders for your main course, side dishes, or appetizers should definitely be a consideration. Still need some convincing? Try the Small-Batch Detroit-Style Pepperoni Pizza (page 143), which is the recipe my friends always request when we get together for movie nights at my place. Looking for a side dish or appetizer instead? Try the Garlic Knots for Two (page 157). Topped with melted garlic butter, parsley, and Parmesan, warm garlic knots are a great side for your soups and chilis. Or make the Cheesy Dinner Rolls (page 153), because who can say no to soft dinner rolls stuffed with melted mozzarella cheese? (No one, that's who!)

So, try a few of the recipes in this chapter out, and then let me know: Which do you prefer, sweet or savory baked goods?

TIPS & TECHNIQUES

INGREDIENT TEMPERATURE: Pay close attention to the temperature of your ingredients. The recipes in this chapter are straightforward and easy to make, but rely heavily on properly softened, warmed, or chilled ingredients. Too-warm butter will make a melty, oily mess of biscuit dough, and you will have a hard time properly mixing butter into dough for pretzels if the butter isn't melted.

KEEP RISING DOUGH WARM: Yeast works best at temperatures between 70°F and 80°F (21°C and 37°C). If your house is cool in the winter, place the bowl somewhere warmer, like the top of a fridge or in a warm (but turned off!) oven. If you put the dough on a heater to rise, insulate the bottom of the bowl with a few fluffy towels. If your house is very warm, the dough may rise more quickly than expected, so keep an eye on it!

SWITCH UP THE SEASONING: Herbs are a great tool for cooking and baking alike; the right spice can elevate a dish from bland to fantastic. With savory baking, recipes can easily be customized to your own preferred flavor profile, so feel free to add, substitute, or omit the various flavors and seasonings as you see fit.

TOTAL TIME:
2 hours 30 minutes

MAKES: 6 slices

FOR THE CRUST

1 cup + 1 tbsp (135 g) bread flour

2¼ tsp (7 g) instant dry yeast

½ tsp fine sea salt

⅓ cup + 1 tsp (85 ml) water

1 tbsp (15 ml) olive oil, plus more for greasing

SMALL-BATCH DETROIT-STYLE PEPPERONI PIZZA

If you've never had Detroit-style pizza before, let me tell you . . . YOU ARE MISSING OUT! Think of Detroit-style pizza as the best possible version of pan pizza. The almost focaccia-like dough gets golden brown and crunchy on the bottom while remaining nice and fluffy in the middle, and it acts as a strong foundation for the hefty amount of cheese, sauce, and, in this case, pepperoni that gets piled on top.

So, you might be wondering how this is different from a pan pizza. First, the pie is sort of built in reverse order: dough, cheese, toppings, and THEN sauce. This allows the crust and cheese to fuse together into one deliciously cheesy, doughy mass. Second, when the sauce finally does make an appearance, it gets draped across the pie in rows. I love this, because adding the sauce on top means you don't have to worry about a soggy crust, and it means that you get a variety of textures and flavors from bite to bite. Last, and maybe most importantly, the cheese goes all the way to the edges of the pan, which means you'll definitely want to fight for an outside piece, because who can resist a crispy, golden brown, cheesy edge?

For the crust, in a large bowl, combine the flour, yeast, and salt. Add the water and oil, and mix with a spatula until a shaggy dough forms and there are no dry bits of flour. The dough will be sticky; this is normal!

Knead the dough on a lightly floured surface until it's elastic, 2 to 4 minutes. Transfer the dough back to the mixing bowl, cover it with plastic wrap, and let it rest for 10 minutes.

Generously drizzle an 8 x 8–inch (20 x 20–cm) nonstick baking pan with olive oil. Turn the dough out into the pan and turn it to fully coat it in the oil. Gently spread and shape the dough into a rough square shape by pressing it down and dimpling the surface with your oiled fingers. The dough won't reach the edges of the pan at this time. Cover the dough with plastic wrap or a kitchen towel, and allow it to rest for 15 minutes.

Uncover the dough, and continue dimpling and stretching the dough with your fingertips. It should be a little more than halfway to the edges of the pan by now. Cover the dough with plastic wrap or a kitchen towel, and allow it to rest for another 15 minutes.

(continued)

FOR THE TOPPINGS

9 oz (255 g) low-moisture mozzarella cheese, cubed

2 oz (50 g) pepperoni cups

½ cup (150 g) pizza sauce

1–2 tbsp (5–10 g) grated Parmesan cheese

Crushed red pepper flakes, to taste

Chopped fresh parsley, optional

Chile-infused hot honey (I like Mike's Hot Honey® brand), optional

SMALL-BATCH DETROIT-STYLE PEPPERONI PIZZA (CONTINUED)

Return to the dough, and dimple and stretch the dough, using extra oil on your hands as needed, until it reaches the edges and corners of the pan. Cover the pan with plastic wrap, and allow the dough to rise for 1 hour. This will be the last rise required! Position an oven rack in the bottom third of the oven and preheat the oven to 500°F (260°C).

Remove the plastic wrap from your dough and, if necessary, coax any dough back into the corners of the pan. The dough will completely fill the bottom of the pan and will look puffy.

For the toppings, evenly add the mozzarella to the surface of the dough, making sure to take it all the way to the edges of the pan.

Top the cheese with the pepperoni cups; be sure to place them overlapping and very close together. It should look like a blanket of pepperoni. Spoon the pizza sauce in even rows on top, leaving some areas without sauce. Top the sauce with the Parmesan and crushed red pepper flakes.

Bake the pizza for 13 to 15 minutes, until the edges are a deep golden brown and the cheese is melted and bubbling on top.

Sprinkle the parsley on top, if using, and allow the pizza to cool in the pan for 5 minutes, then carefully remove the pizza to a cutting board. Slice it into pieces with a pizza cutter or sharp knife and top it with the hot honey, if using.

***

COOKING TIP: *Detroit-style pizza is typically baked in a special dark anodized pan to achieve the perfectly crispy caramelized cheese around the edge, but a standard baking pan works well, too; the darker the pan, the better!*

MAKES: One 8 x 8–inch
(20 x 20–cm) focaccia

FOR THE FOCACCIA

2½ cups (318 g) bread flour

2¼ tsp (7 g) instant dry yeast

1 tsp granulated sugar

1 tsp fine sea salt

1 cup + 3 tbsp (285 ml) water,
warm (115°F [45°C])

3 tbsp (45 ml) olive oil, divided,
plus more as needed

SMALL–BATCH GARLIC & ROSEMARY FOCACCIA

I'm kind of in love with focaccia. It amazes me how just a few simple ingredients—flour, yeast, salt, and water—can make such a delicious product. What amazes me more is how easy it is to actually make. If you want to fill your kitchen with the smell of fresh-baked bread, but you're nervous about shaping a boule or working with a sourdough starter, focaccia is the best place to begin. You can make this in one bowl with a single spatula—or just your hands—and there's no kneading involved! And, even if you skip the garlic and rosemary topping, this will still make for a fantastic sandwich bread.

For the focaccia, in a large bowl, combine the flour, yeast, sugar, and salt. Add the water, and mix it in with a spatula until a dough forms and there are no dry pockets of flour. The dough will be *extremely* wet and sticky. Cover the bowl with plastic wrap; let the dough rest for 5 minutes.

Perform a set of stretches and folds on the dough. To do this, wet your hands, then take a section of the dough near the edge of the bowl, stretch it up, and fold it onto itself. Rotate the bowl 90 degrees and repeat the process. Repeat this process six more times, until you have gone around the bowl twice (a total of eight stretches and folds). Cover the bowl with plastic wrap, and let the dough rest for 5 minutes. Repeat the stretching, folding, and resting process two more times, for a total of three rounds of stretches and folds, each 5 minutes apart; cover the bowl with plastic wrap for each rest period.

Drizzle the surface of the dough with 1 tablespoon (15 ml) of the olive oil, and turn the dough over in the bowl to coat it with the oil. Cover the bowl with plastic wrap, then allow the dough to rise until it's doubled in size, 60 to 90 minutes.

Grease an 8 x 8–inch (20 x 20–cm) pan with butter or coat it with nonstick cooking spray. (Note: This greasing step may seem excessive, but with some pans, it is imperative to do so to prevent sticking.) Pour 1 tablespoon (15 ml) of oil into the center of the pan, and then turn the risen dough out into the pan. Pour any oil left in the bowl on top of the dough, turn it to fully coat the dough in oil, then let the dough rest for 5 minutes.

(continued)

2 tbsp (30 ml) olive oil

4 cloves garlic, minced

1 sprig rosemary leaves

Flaky sea salt

SMALL-BATCH GARLIC & ROSEMARY FOCACCIA (CONTINUED)

Gently spread the dough toward the edges of the pan, using your fingers; it doesn't have to reach all the way. Drizzle the surface of the dough with an additional tablespoon (15 ml) of oil, and let it rise, uncovered, in a dry, warm spot until it's doubled in size, at least 1½ hours or up to 4 hours. To see if the dough is ready, poke it with your finger. It should spring back slowly, leaving a small visible indentation. If it springs back quickly, the dough isn't ready. (If at this point the dough is ready to bake but you aren't, you can chill it for up to 1 hour.)

Toward the end of the rising process, place a rack in the middle of the oven and preheat it to 450°F (230°C).

To prepare the toppings, stir the olive oil and garlic in a small bowl to combine the ingredients. Spoon the mixture evenly over the surface of the dough.

Rub your hands lightly in oil to coat, then, using all of your fingers, press straight down to create deep dimples all over the surface of the dough; if bubbles form in the dough, do not pop them. If necessary, gently stretch the dough as you dimple to allow the dough to fill the pan. Sprinkle the dough all over with the rosemary and salt.

Bake the focaccia for 25 to 30 minutes, or until it is puffed, golden brown on the surface, and pulling away from the sides of the pan. Allow the focaccia to rest in the pan for 5 minutes, then remove it, and cool it on a wire rack. (Don't let the focaccia cool completely in the pan, otherwise you could end up with a soggy bottom.)

Focaccia is best eaten the day it's made, but it keeps well in the freezer. To freeze, cut the focaccia into squares and place the pieces on a parchment-paper lined baking sheet so they have space between them. Put the baking sheet in the freezer for up to 2 hours, then wrap the focaccia pieces in plastic wrap, place them in freezer bags, and freeze for up to 1 month.

To reheat the focaccia, preheat the oven to 375°F (190°C). Allow the focaccia to defrost for a few hours at room temperature, then place it on a parchment-paper lined baking sheet. Mist the focaccia with water using a spray bottle, then bake it for 6 to 8 minutes.

MAKE-AHEAD INSTRUCTIONS: *To make the night before you want to serve the focaccia, prepare the dough up until the first rise, then cover the dough tightly with plastic wrap, and refrigerate it for a minimum of 12 hours or up to 2 days. When you are ready to resume the recipe, proceed with the rest of the instructions. If you perform your first rise overnight in the fridge, your second rise at room temperature will be closer to the 4-hour mark.*

TOTAL TIME: 45 minutes

MAKES: 6 biscuits

FOR THE BISCUITS

2 cups (240 g) all-purpose flour

1½ tbsp (22 g) baking powder

¾ tsp fine sea salt

6 tbsp (85 g) unsalted butter, cold and cubed

⅔ cup + 2 tbsp (190 ml) buttermilk, cold and divided

½ tbsp (10 g) honey

Turbinado sugar, for sprinkling

FOR THE HONEY BUTTER GLAZE

1 tbsp (14 g) unsalted butter, melted

½ tbsp (10 g) honey

⅛ tsp fine sea salt

COOKING TIP: *Not sure if your biscuits are done? With a fork or spatula, gently lift one and look at the bottom. If the bottom is nicely browned, it's time to take them out of the oven!*

HONEY BUTTERMILK BISCUITS

I have become a total biscuit snob. They have to be just right—crisp on the outside, and fluffy and flaky on the inside. The baking powder flavor can't be overpowering, and they have to be buttery and melt-in-your-mouth tender. These Honey Buttermilk Biscuits are both delicious and versatile. You can serve them alongside dinner, make them into breakfast sandwiches, or turn them into strawberry shortcakes.

Preheat the oven to 425°F (220°C). Line a baking sheet with parchment paper, and set aside the pan.

To make the biscuits, in a medium bowl, whisk together the flour, baking powder, and salt to combine. Add the butter, tossing the cubes through the flour until each individual piece is well coated. Working quickly, using a pastry cutter or your fingers, cut the butter into the flour until the butter is about the size of walnut halves.

Make a well in the center of the flour mixture, and add ⅔ cup + 1 tablespoon (175 ml) of the buttermilk and the honey. Using a silicone spatula, fold everything to combine the ingredients, until the dough begins to come together. Be careful not to overwork the dough! It will be shaggy and crumbly with some wet spots.

Pour the dough and any dry crumbles onto a floured work surface, and gently bring them together, using generously floured hands. The dough will become sticky as you bring it together. Have extra flour nearby, and use it often to flour your hands and your work surface, so that nothing sticks.

Using a rolling pin or floured hands, roll out/flatten the dough into a ¾-inch (2-cm)-thick rectangle (the exact size doesn't matter, just the thickness). Brush off any excess flour with a dry pastry brush, then fold the dough into thirds like a letter. Rotate the dough 90 degrees, and gently roll out/flatten it into a ¾-inch (2-cm)-thick rectangle and repeat the folding. Repeat the rotating, rolling, and folding process one more time.

Flatten the dough into a ¾-inch (2-cm)-thick rectangle approximately 9 x 5–inches (23 x 13–cm), and trim a thin border around the sides of the dough to create clean edges. Using a knife or bench scraper, cut the dough into a 3 x 2 grid to make six biscuits. Place the biscuits close together, about ½ inch (1.3 cm) apart, on the prepared baking sheet. Brush the tops with the remaining 1 tablespoon (15 ml) of buttermilk, and sprinkle the tops with the turbinado sugar. Bake the biscuits for 15 to 17 minutes, or until the tops are golden brown.

While the biscuits are baking, prepare the glaze. In a small bowl, stir together the butter, honey, and salt until combined. Once you remove the biscuits from the oven, carefully brush the tops with the honey butter, and serve them warm. Cover leftovers tightly, and store them at room temperature or in the refrigerator for up to 4 days.

TOTAL TIME: 30 minutes

MAKES: 6 muffins

⅔ cup (83 g) all-purpose flour

½ cup (75 g) yellow cornmeal, see Ingredient Tip

6 tbsp (75 g) granulated sugar

2 tsp (10 g) baking powder

¼ tsp fine sea salt

⅓ cup (75 ml) canola oil

1 large egg, room temperature

½ cup (120 ml) milk, room temperature

SWEET CORNBREAD MUFFINS

This next statement might get some Southern folks riled up, but it's the cold, hard truth. I like sugar in my cornbread (cue the gasps and pearl clutching). For me, cornbread is sort of a complement to the meal, and I like it a little sweet—like Jiffy Corn Muffin Mix sweet. And, while I do love me some Jiffy, I don't always remember to grab that little blue and white box at the grocery store. So, I make them from scratch and that's the recipe you see before you now. The best part? It's a one-bowl recipe that comes together in no time at all.

Preheat the oven to 400°F (200°C). Spray a 6-cup muffin pan with nonstick spray, then set aside the pan.

In a large bowl, whisk together the flour, cornmeal, sugar, baking powder, and salt until combined. In a medium bowl, whisk together the oil, egg, and milk. Add the wet ingredients to the dry ingredients, and whisk everything together gently, just until the ingredients are combined and no flour pockets remain.

Spoon the batter into the prepared muffin pan, filling each cup almost full; you'll use about 4 tablespoons (70 g) of batter per cup. Bake the muffins for 15 minutes, or until a toothpick inserted into the center comes out clean. Allow the muffins to cool for 10 minutes in the muffin pan before removing them to a wire rack to cool completely.

Cover leftover muffins tightly, and store them at room temperature for up to 2 days.

INGREDIENT TIP: *Choose a fine- or medium-grind cornmeal. A medium grind will give you some texture, while a fine grind will yield muffins with a denser crumb.*

MAKES: 4 rolls

1 cup (120 g) all-purpose flour

2¼ tsp (7 g) instant dry yeast

½ tsp fine sea salt

¼ tsp garlic powder

¼ tsp onion powder

2 tbsp + 1 tsp (35 ml) water, warm (115°F [45°C])

2 tbsp + 1 tsp (35 ml) milk, warm (115°F [45°C])

1 tbsp (14 g) unsalted butter, melted

1 tbsp (15 ml) olive oil

2 oz (56 g) mozzarella cheese, shredded and divided

1 tbsp (5 g) grated Parmesan cheese

1 tsp Italian seasoning

CHEESY DINNER ROLLS

These cheesy dinner rolls are soft and fluffy yeast rolls filled with gooey chunks of mozzarella cheese and seasoned with Italian herbs and garlic. They're like the love child of mozzarella sticks and Parker house rolls, and I'm not even remotely mad about it. Although they're delicious on their own, try serving them alongside a tangy marinara sauce for dipping for a true treat!

In the bowl of a stand mixer, whisk together the flour, yeast, salt, garlic powder, and onion powder. Add the water, milk, butter, and olive oil. Using the hook attachment, knead the dough on medium speed for about 5 minutes until a soft dough forms. Increase the speed to medium-high, and beat until the dough is soft and supple and pulls away from the sides of the bowl, about 5 minutes. The dough will be very soft, but not overly sticky. Beat in 1 to 2 more tablespoons (8 to 15 g) of flour if the dough seems very sticky; avoid adding more flour than you need. If you do not have a stand mixer with a hook attachment, knead the dough by hand in this step.

Transfer the dough to a lightly floured surface, and knead it with your hands for 1 minute. Form the dough into a ball, and transfer it back to the mixing bowl. Cover the dough loosely with plastic wrap; let it sit in a warm place until it's doubled in size, about 60 minutes.

Grease a baking dish or 6-inch (15-cm) cake pan.

Turn the dough out onto a lightly floured work surface, then weigh the dough. Divide it into four equal-sized pieces and shape them into balls. Flatten each ball into a circle with your fingers. Place ½ ounce (14 g) of shredded mozzarella cheese in the middle. Fold the perimeter of the dough over the cheese, and pinch the edges together to close the dough around the filling. Place the balls in the greased baking dish about ½ inch (1.3 cm) apart. Cover the pan, and allow the rolls to proof for 25 to 30 minutes.

While the rolls are rising, preheat the oven to 375°F (190°C). Once proofed, lightly brush the tops with water and sprinkle on the Parmesan cheese and Italian seasoning. Bake the rolls for 20 to 25 minutes, or until golden brown. Allow the rolls to cool slightly before serving.

Store leftovers in an airtight container for up to 1 day. To reheat room-temperature rolls, wrap them in aluminum foil, place them on a baking sheet, and bake in a 350°F (180°C) oven for 10 minutes.

TOTAL TIME: 30 minutes

MAKES: 6–8 biscuits

FOR THE BISCUITS

1 cup (120 g) all-purpose flour

1 tbsp (12 g) granulated sugar

½ tbsp (8 g) baking powder

1 tsp garlic powder

¼ tsp onion powder

½ tsp fine sea salt

½ cup (120 ml) buttermilk

¼ cup (57 g) unsalted butter, melted

1 cup (115 g) freshly grated Cheddar cheese

FOR THE GARLIC BUTTER TOPPING

3 tbsp (40 g) unsalted butter, melted

½ tbsp (1 g) chopped fresh parsley

¼ tsp garlic powder

⅛ tsp fine sea salt

CHEDDAR BAY BISCUITS

Truth be told, I prefer just about anything over seafood. Oddly enough though, Red Lobster is one of my favorite restaurants. If you have ever been there with me, you know I can just about eat my body weight in Cheddar Bay Biscuits. So, it was a no-brainer to try and come up with my own copycat version. These beautifully light, flaky, garlicky cheddar drop biscuits glisten with butter and are speckled with parsley; they are slightly crisp on the outside and perfectly tender on the inside. I am in Cheddar Bay heaven. The best part is they only require one bowl, one whisk, and 30 minutes.

Preheat the oven to 450°F (230°C). Line a baking sheet with parchment paper, and set aside the pan.

In a medium bowl, whisk together the flour, sugar, baking powder, garlic powder, onion powder, and salt to combine. Make a well in the center of the dry ingredients, and add the buttermilk and butter. Stir, using a rubber spatula, just until moist. Gently fold in the cheese.

Using a large (3-tablespoon [42-g]) spring-loaded scoop, portion out the biscuits, and place them evenly on the prepared baking sheet. Bake the biscuits for 10 to 12 minutes, or until light golden brown.

While the biscuits are baking, prepare the garlic butter topping. In a small bowl, whisk together the butter, parsley, garlic powder, and salt. Brush the tops of the biscuits with the butter mixture as soon as you remove them from the oven. Serve the biscuits immediately.

Store leftovers in an airtight container in the refrigerator. To reheat, wrap the biscuits in foil, and bake them for 6 to 7 minutes in a 350°F (180°F) oven, until they are warmed through.

TOTAL TIME: 3 hours

MAKES: 8 knots

FOR THE BRIOCHE DOUGH

1¾ cups (220 g) all-purpose flour

2¼ tsp (7 g) instant dry yeast

1 tsp granulated sugar

¼ tsp garlic powder

¼ tsp fine sea salt

⅔ cup (160 ml) water, warm (115°F [45°C])

1 tbsp (15 ml) olive oil

FOR THE GARLIC BUTTER TOPPING

¼ cup (57 g) unsalted butter, melted

4 garlic cloves, minced

½ tsp Italian seasoning

⅛ tsp fine sea salt

2 tbsp (10 g) grated Parmesan

1 tbsp (2 g) chopped fresh parsley

FOR SERVING

Marinara sauce, optional

GARLIC KNOTS FOR TWO

I'm trying to think of something more delicious than warm garlic knots fresh out of the oven. . . . And, I'm giving up. It's just not possible. Garlic knots deliver everything you love about dinner rolls—soft! fluffy!—plus an extra kick of rich, savory garlic flavor. Because they can pass as an appetizer, snack, or even a side dish with the right meal, there's never an occasion where they're out of place.

For the dough, in the bowl of a stand mixer or in a large mixing bowl, whisk together the flour, yeast, sugar, garlic powder, and salt. Add the water and olive oil, and mix until the ingredients are just barely combined. Let the mixture stand for 5 minutes so the flour has time to hydrate.

Using the hook attachment, knead the dough on medium speed for about 5 minutes until a soft dough forms. Increase the speed to medium-high, and beat until the dough is soft and supple and pulls away from the sides of the bowl, about 5 minutes. The dough will be very soft, but not overly sticky. Beat in 1 to 2 more tablespoons (8 to 15 g) of flour if the dough seems very sticky; avoid adding more flour than you need. If you do not have a stand mixer with a hook attachment, knead the dough by hand in this step.

Transfer the dough to a lightly floured surface, and knead it with your hands for 1 minute. Form the dough into a ball, and transfer it back to the mixing bowl. Cover the dough loosely with plastic wrap, and let it sit in a warm place until it's doubled in size, 45 to 60 minutes.

While the dough is rising, prepare the topping. In a small bowl, whisk together the butter, garlic, Italian seasoning, and salt, then set aside the mixture. Line a baking sheet with parchment paper; set it aside.

When the dough is ready, punch it down to release the air. Weigh the dough. Using a sharp knife or bench scraper, divide it into 8 even portions. Roll each strip into 8-inch (20-cm) ropes, and then tie each one into knots. You can tuck the two ends of the knots underneath the knot or leave them out; that's up to you. Arrange the knots on the prepared baking sheet. Lightly cover the knots with plastic wrap and let them proof for 30 to 45 minutes, or until they are risen and puffed.

While the knots are proofing, preheat the oven to 400°F (200°C). Brush some of the garlic butter topping on the knots; reserve some of the topping for when the knots come out of the oven. Bake the knots for 20 to 22 minutes, or until they are golden brown on top. Remove the knots from the oven, and brush them with the remaining garlic butter. Sprinkle the Parmesan cheese and parsley on top. Serve the knots plain or with the marinara sauce, for dipping.

Cover and store leftover knots at room temperature for up to 2 days or in the refrigerator for up to 1 week.

TOTAL TIME:
2 hours 30 minutes

MAKES: 4 pretzels

FOR THE SOFT PRETZELS

½ cup (120 ml) milk, warm (115°F [45°C])

2¼ tsp (7 g) instant dry yeast

1 tbsp (12 g) granulated sugar

½ tsp fine sea salt

1 tbsp (14 g) unsalted butter, melted

1½ cups (180 g) all-purpose flour

Pretzel salt or coarse sea salt, for sprinkling

SOFT PRETZELS WITH SPICY CHEESE DIP

While the thought of soft pretzels might leave you reminiscing about your teen years at the mall or amusement park, once you make them at home, you'll never go back to the food court again! Most pretzels in the world are made with lye, which gives pretzels their signature chewy, brown crust. However, lye can be hard to find and a bit dangerous for people who aren't careful when handling it, which is why this recipe opts for a baking soda bath. When you dissolve the baking soda in boiling water, the alkalinity of the baking soda solution allows the exterior of the pretzel to brown at a significantly faster rate, giving it that signature crust and flavor. I mean, seriously, what's better than fresh homemade soft pretzels and a bowl of creamy, silky, spicy cheese sauce? Nothing . . . that's what!

For the pretzels, in the bowl of a stand mixer fitted with the dough hook attachment, whisk together the milk, yeast, and sugar. Allow the mixture to sit for 5 minutes, or until it's foamy/bubbly. Whisk in the salt and butter, then add the flour, and mix on low for 2 to 3 minutes, until the dough begins to come together. Increase the speed to medium, and knead the dough for 10 minutes, until the dough is smooth and stretchy. Beat in 1 to 2 more tablespoons (8 to 15 g) of flour if the dough seems very sticky; avoid adding more flour than you need. Shape the dough into a ball, and transfer it back to the mixing bowl. Cover the dough with plastic wrap, and allow it to rise in a warm spot for 45 to 60 minutes, or until it's doubled in size.

Line a baking sheet with parchment paper or a silicone baking mat. If using parchment paper, lightly spray it with nonstick spray or grease it with butter. Set aside the pan.

Turn the dough out onto a lightly floured work surface, then weigh the dough. Divide it into 4 equal-sized balls. Cover three balls of dough with plastic wrap. Working with one piece of dough at a time, roll the dough into a 20- to 22-inch (50- to 55-cm) rope. Take the ends and draw them upward so the dough forms a U. Twist the ends, then bring them toward yourself and press them down into a pretzel shape. Transfer the pretzel to the lined baking sheet. Repeat the process with the remaining dough balls, until you have four pretzels spaced evenly on the baking sheet. Allow the pretzels to rise, uncovered, at room temperature for 20 minutes, then refrigerate them for 10 to 15 minutes. While the pretzels rise, preheat the oven to 400°F (200°C), and prepare the baking soda bath.

(continued)

SOFT PRETZELS WITH SPICY CHEESE DIP (CONTINUED)

FOR THE BAKING SODA BATH

3 cups (720 ml) water

1½ tbsp (23 g) baking soda

FOR THE SPICY CHEESE DIP

2 tbsp (28 g) unsalted butter

2 tbsp (15 g) all-purpose flour

1 cup (240 ml) milk

1 cup (115 g) freshly grated Cheddar cheese

1 tsp Sriracha, see Ingredient Tip

½ tsp red pepper flakes

⅛ tsp cayenne pepper, see Ingredient Tip

Salt and pepper, to taste

Bring the water and baking soda to a boil in a large pot. Once the pretzels have risen, remove them from the fridge, and, working with one pretzel at a time, drop the pretzel into the boiling water for 20 to 30 seconds. (Any more than that and your pretzels will have a metallic taste, so be careful!) Using a slotted spatula, lift the pretzel out of the water, and allow as much of the excess water to drip off as possible. Place the pretzel back onto the prepared baking sheet and sprinkle it with the salt. Repeat with the remaining pretzels. Bake the pretzels for 10 to 12 minutes, or until they are golden brown.

While the pretzels are baking, prepare the cheese sauce. Melt the butter in a saucepan over medium heat. Sprinkle the flour on top, and whisk constantly until a thick paste forms, 1 to 2 minutes. Slowly stream the milk into the saucepan, whisking constantly. Continue whisking and cooking until the mixture thickens, 4 to 5 minutes. It should be thick, but still pourable. Add the cheese and whisk constantly until it's melted. Add the Sriracha, red pepper flakes, and cayenne pepper. Add salt and pepper to taste.

The cheese sauce will thicken upon cooling. Store leftovers, covered tightly, in the refrigerator for up to 5 days. Heat it on the stove or in the microwave before serving it.

Cover and store leftover pretzels at room temperature for up to 3 days. They lose a little softness over time. To reheat, microwave for a few seconds or bake in a 350°F (180°C) oven for 5 minutes.

INGREDIENT TIP: *Feel free to adjust the spiciness to your liking by either adding more Sriracha and cayenne pepper or by omitting them completely!*

MAKE-AHEAD INSTRUCTIONS: *To make the night before serving, prepare the dough up until the first rise, then cover the dough tightly with plastic wrap, and refrigerate it for a minimum of 8 hours or up to 16 hours. When you are ready to resume the recipe, proceed with the instructions. Note: If you perform your first rise overnight in the fridge, your second rise at room temperature will take slightly longer, 45 minutes to 1 hour.*

ACKNOWLEDGMENTS

I'd first and foremost like to thank my mom, Angela, and grandparents, Richard and Marsha, who have always been my biggest cheerleaders. Thank you for encouraging me to follow my dreams.

To the entire team at Page Street Publishing Co., especially Madeline Greenhalgh and Meg Baskis: This was our second time around, and I couldn't have been happier to work with you again! Thank you for your hard work and support.

To SMITH&SAINT, specifically Madison: Thank you for helping me keep the bills paid and lights on at Mike Bakes NYC while I poured everything into this book. You helped keep my scatterbrain on top of projects and deadlines, and I'm SO grateful for your management.

To my incredible group of recipe testers: I'm eternally grateful for your volunteering to help test my recipes. Through a callout on social media, I ended up with 400+ volunteers that I had to impossibly narrow down to just 30 people who ultimately baked their way through this entire book. Thank you for your invaluable time and feedback.

To my fellow food bloggers, especially Ari, Erin, and Kylie, who I constantly badgered with recipe titles, photos to choose between, complaints, and more, thank you!

To my best friends, Alodie, Sam, Esther, Stephen, Taylor, and Janae: Thank you for your words of encouragement throughout the entire cookbook process and for always helping keep me sane.

And last, but certainly not least, to all the readers and followers of Mike Bakes NYC: Thank you for baking along with me. Your support allows me to do what I'm passionate about, and there's nothing I love more than seeing you guys make my recipes and share them with loved ones. None of this would be possible without you!

ABOUT THE AUTHOR

Mike Johnson is the baker, photographer, and blogger behind the sweets-focused blog Mike Bakes NYC and the author of *Even Better Brownies*. His work has appeared on- and offline in *Bake from Scratch* magazine, BuzzFeed, Food52, and the *New York Times*. He currently lives in New York City.

INDEX